200 veggie

200 veggie feasts

hamlyn **all color**

Louise Pickford

An Hachette Livre UK company
www.hachettelivre.co.uk

First published in Great Britain in 2008 by Hamlyn,
a division of Octopus Publishing Group Ltd
2–4 Heron Quays, London E14 4JP
www.octopusbooksusa.com

Distributed in the U.S. and Canada by Octopus Books USA:
c/o Hachette Book Group USA
237 Park Avenue
New York NY 10017

Some of the recipes in this book have previously
appeared in the following books published by Hamlyn:
15-minute Feasts, *30-minute Entertaining* by Louise Pickford

ISBN: 978-0-600-61872-0

A CIP catalog record for this book is available from the
Library of Congress

Printed and bound in China

1 2 3 4 5 6 7 8 9 10

Standard level spoon measurements are used in all recipes.

Ovens should be preheated to the specified temperature. If
using a fan-assisted oven, follow the manufacturer's
instructions for adjusting the time and temperature.

The varieties of cheese used in this book may not always
be strictly vegetarian, but many cheeses are available in
vegetarian form. Always check the label so that you know
what you are buying.

Eggs should be medium unless otherwise stated; choose free-
range if possible and preferably organic. The Food and Drug
Administration advises that eggs should not be consumed
raw. This book contains some dishes made with raw or lightly
cooked eggs. It is prudent for more vulnerable people, such
as pregnant and nursing mothers, invalids, the elderly, babies,
and young children, to avoid uncooked or lightly cooked
dishes made with eggs.

This book includes dishes made with nuts and nut derivatives.
It is advisable for those with known allergic reactions to
nuts and nut derivatives and those who may be potentially
vulnerable to these allergies, such as pregnant and nursing
mothers, invalids, the elderly, babies, and children, to avoid
dishes made with nuts and nut oils.

contents

introduction

introduction

Today, choosing to eat a vegetarian diet is far easier than it ever was, with such high-quality and varied produce to choose from in our supermarkets and food stores. Whether you are a vegetarian yourself, cooking for a vegetarian, or just looking for some inspirational meat-free recipes to enjoy from time to time, this book is packed with exciting and innovative ideas for everyday meals. Each recipe is expertly photographed so that you can see exactly what you will be cooking, and every one offers a creative variation, giving a total of 200 recipes in one handy package!

time factor

Because time is so precious to us in our modern hectic world, getting a meal on the

table as speedily as possible is paramount, and this book has been specifically designed with that in mind, offering a wide range of versatile quick-and-easy dishes. Since many of these delicious recipes can be prepared and cooked in 30 minutes or less, any lingering concern you may have that vegetarian food is more involved and time-consuming to cook than meat-based food, will soon be consigned to myth.

To help us cook more efficiently, we need to shop well, so that everything we require is on hand or can be bought on the way home from work. If you forward plan your week, shopping for staples and nonperishables in one go, you can then simply pick up fresh ingredients as and when you need them. A well-stocked pantry is invaluable, so make sure you always have the basics at your fingertips, such as extra virgin olive oil, balsamic vinegar, sea salt, canned tomatoes and beans, dried lentils, pasta, rice, and flour.

healthy choices

Although a vegetarian diet doesn't guarantee better health, any risk associated with eating red meat is obviously eliminated. Unless you are vegan, you will most likely be consuming other animal products, including eggs, cheese, butter, cream, and milk, but it is important to avoid the common trap of overcompensating

processed foods. Always purchase fruit, vegetables, and herbs in the best, freshest condition possible to gain the maximum nutritional benefits. There is a far greater choice now when it comes to buying organic, but it remains the more expensive option. It is always worthwhile purchasing organic free-range eggs, but beyond that, you can choose which organic produce to buy according to your budget and what looks best on the day.

And remember that the only sure-fire way of knowing exactly what we are eating is to make our meals ourselves. So start cooking now and enjoy some really fabulous vegetarian food.

storing fresh ingredients

Once you have bought the best-quality ingredients it is important to use them as soon as possible, or to store them so that they maintain as much freshness as possible.

Most fruits and vegetables should be kept in the refrigerator, but those that don't chill—such as potatoes, onions, garlic, apples, and other high-starch foods—should be kept in a cool dark place, preferably in paper bags.

Unless you have bought herbs in pots, I find the best method for keeping them perky is to place them in a large zip-lock bag with a sprinkle of cold water. Seal the bag and store in the refrigerator.

for the lack of meat by consuming, in particular, large quantities of cheese, which is high in saturated fats that can lead to heart disease. A balanced diet is vital in providing our bodies with the right amount of proteins, carbohydrates, essential fats, vitamins, and minerals to maintain good health. We can do this by eating plenty of fresh fruit and vegetables (the recommended daily intake is at least five servings per day), as well as legumes, grains, and soybean products combined with sensible amounts of eggs, milk, and cheese.

To get the most from our food, we need to buy good-quality fresh ingredients and avoid

recipes for every occasion

The book is divided into seven chapters, designed to make choosing the type of dish you want to cook ultra easy. If you are looking for a snack or a main meal, a side salad and a dessert, each recipe can be found in its respective chapter. Planning a dinner party? You can quickly put a menu together by searching through the appropriate chapters to find exactly what you want. And with a useful variation for each recipe, you have double the choice.

Vegetarian options may seem limited for **breakfast & brunch**, but here you will find lots of delicious ideas to nourish and satisfy any discerning diner. Try the wickedly rich and indulgent Arugula & Goat Cheese Omelet (see page 18) or feed family and friends in laid-back style with the washing-up

friendly All-In-One Veggie Breakfast (see page 22).

Many of the great-tasting dishes in **appetizers & snacks** will suit either role, making them particularly versatile. There are several that can be ready to eat in less than 20 minutes, such as the rather exotic-sounding Haloumi with Pomegranate Salsa (see page 42) or the Bean, Lemon, & Rosemary Hummus (see page 68)—a delicious bean pâté.

What you will find surprisingly refreshing about the **main meals** chapter is that many of the recipes are not stereotypically vegetarian. Rather, they are dishes that meat-eaters and non-meat-eaters alike will yearn for and eat regularly, such as the Creamy Pea & Mint Risotto with Brie (see page 80), Spinach & Ricotta Cannelloni (see page 100), or Fava Bean & Lemon Spaghetti (see page 82).

The **soups & stews** chapter features quick-and-easy soup recipes suitable for everyday family meals, as well as others that would make the perfect appetizer to any dinner party, such as the indulgent Mushroom Soup with Truffle Butter (see page 112). A few of the dishes are more substantial stews, ideal for a chilly winter's night—for example, the wonderfully hearty Goulash with Chive Dumplings (see page 130).

In **salads & sides** you will find some enduring classics, but most dishes offer a

modern twist on the more traditional recipe, such as Roast Vegetables & Parsley Pesto (see page 160) or the Baked Sweet Potatoes (see page 166), filled with sour cream and chives. Some of the dishes make great accompaniments to main meals, while others could provide a tasty light lunch.

There is something wonderfully comforting about the thought of home baking and you will find a whole variety of enticing recipes in **breads & baking**. The heavenly smell of freshly baked bread is hard to beat and what better way to ensure a delicious supper than to bake a savory tart. You will be amazed at just how easy it is to make your own pizzas— the Roasted Squash & Sage Pizza (see page 192) is a revelation!

Last, but never least, is a chapter on **desserts**, because we all need to indulge from time to time in some of the sweeter

things in life. Why not try the simple but totally divine Rich Chocolate Mousse (see page 200), so easy to make that you won't believe it. Or for a really special occasion, perhaps when friends are over for dinner, make the Tiramisù Cheesecake (see page 212)—those familiar flavors never tasted so good.

ingredients guide

The following are some useful, practical notes on some of the ingredients featured in the recipes, including the more unusual items.

eggs

Always buy free-range, preferably organic eggs. If you keep your eggs in the refrigerator, always remove them and leave at room temperature for 1 hour before use.

buttermilk

This is the liquid that remains after cream is churned into butter. Similar to milk but with less fat and a slightly sour taste, it is a great alternative to both milk and yogurt, and can be found in the chill cabinet in supermarkets and health-food stores.

haloumi cheese

A hard, salty sheep's milk cheese from Cyprus, haloumi is always eaten cooked and should be consumed as soon as it melts, as it can become rather chewy when it cools.

fontina cheese

This is a mild Italian cows' milk cheese that melts really well. You can also substitute mozzarella cheese, which has a milder flavor. Fontina is available from some of

the larger supermarkets, Italian delis, and specialty food stores.

taleggio cheese

This soft Italian cows' milk cheese is similar to Brie, which could be used instead. It is available from cheese stores, Italian delis, and some larger supermarkets.

arborio rice

A medium-grain rice grown in Italy, arborio is traditionally used to make risotto, as its high starch content adds a creamy consistency to the finished dish. It is widely available.

polenta

An Italian maize-like porridge, polenta can be served soft or left to set, cut into squares, and chargrilled. The grain itself is known as cornmeal, which you can use instead. Instant polenta is used in the recipes in this book.

ramen noodles

These are traditional Japanese dried noodles available from Asian markets. There are several types of dried noodles used in Japanese soups, and you can choose any of these for the recipes in this book.

savoiardi cookies

These thin, finger-shaped cookies topped with sugar are traditionally used to make tiramisù. They are the Italian version of ladyfingers.

herbs

Always use fresh herbs whenever possible. If you have to use dried herbs, use half the amount specified in the ingredients list. Why not buy some potted herbs and keep on the windowsill for a cheaper option?

kaffir lime leaves

These are the fragrant leaves of the Kaffir lime tree. They are used extensively in Thai cooking and are available fresh from good greengrocers, Asian markets, and some supermarkets. You can freeze fresh leaves and use them straight from the freezer.

vegetable stock

Always use a good-quality vegetable stock. Often bouillon powders are superior to stock cubes, but it is best to try out several varieties to find the one you like best.

vincotto

This is an Italian condiment made from dried grape must that is boiled to a thick syrup and aged in oak barrels. It is similar to aged balsamic vinegar. It is available from some Italian delis, specialty food stores, and internet suppliers.

marsala

This is a fortified wine from Sicily with a deep color and wonderful spicy aroma. It is the traditional flavoring in tiramisù and also makes a delicious aperitif.

tahini paste

Made from ground sesame seeds, this paste is used extensively in North African cooking and is widely available from health-food stores.

mirin

This is a spirit-based, sweet liquid used in Japanese cooking, and is available from larger supermarkets, Asian markets, and health-food stores.

wakame seaweed

This dried seaweed is used in Japanese cooking, and adds a deep flavor to stocks and soups. It is available from health-food stores.

breakfast &
brunch

parmesan eggy bread

Serves **6**
Preparation time **10 minutes**
Cooking time **8–14 minutes**

6 **plum tomatoes**
4 tablespoons ready-made
   olive tapenade
extra virgin olive oil, for
   drizzling
⅔ cup **milk**
3 **eggs**
3 tablespoons freshly grated
   Parmesan cheese
¼ cup **butter**
6 slices of **white bread**
handful of **baby spinach**
   leaves
a few **basil leaves**, to serve
salt and black pepper

Cut the tomatoes in half and scoop out the seeds.
Arrange cut-side up in a baking dish. Spoon a little of
the tapenade onto each tomato and drizzle over some
oil. Cook under a preheated hot broiler for 2–3 minutes
until soft and golden. Keep warm.

Beat the milk, eggs, Parmesan, and a little salt and
pepper together in a bowl. Pour into a shallow dish.
Melt half the butter in a large skillet. Dip 3 bread slices
into the egg mixture, add to the pan and fry over a
medium heat for 3–4 minutes, turning once, until
golden on both sides. Remove and keep warm in a
moderate oven. Repeat with the remaining bread slices
and egg mixture.

Serve the eggy bread topped with the broiled
tomatoes, baby spinach leaves, and a few basil leaves.

For sweet eggy bread, dip 4 slices of brioche
into a mixture of 2 beaten eggs, 2 tablespoons
superfine sugar, and ½ teaspoon ground cinnamon.
Melt 2 tablespoons butter in a skillet, add half the
bread slices and fry for 2–3 minutes on each side
until golden. Repeat with the remaining brioche
slices and egg mixture. Serve the bread dusted
with confectioners' sugar, topped with fresh berries
and a dollop of whipped cream.

arugula & goat cheese omelet

Serves **4**
Preparation time **5 minutes**
Cooking time **12 minutes**

12 **eggs**
4 tablespoons **milk**
4 tablespoons chopped
  mixed herbs, such as
  chervil, chives, marjoram,
  parsley, and tarragon
¼ cup **butter**
4 oz **soft goat cheese**, diced
small handful of **baby arugula
  leaves**
salt and black pepper

Beat the eggs, milk, herbs, and salt and pepper together in a large bowl. Melt a quarter of the butter in an omelet pan. As soon as it stops foaming, swirl in a quarter of the egg mixture and cook over a medium heat, forking over the omelet so that it cooks evenly.

As soon as it is set on the underside, but still a little runny in the center, sprinkle a quarter of the cheese and a quarter of the arugula leaves over one half of the omelet. Carefully slide the omelet onto a warmed serving plate, folding it in half as you go. For the best results, serve immediately, then repeat to make 3 more omelets and serve each individually. Alternatively, keep warm in a moderate oven and serve all together.

For cheese & tomato omelet, follow the recipe above to the end of the first stage. Then top each omelet with 2 tablespoons grated cheddar cheese and 2 halved cherry tomatoes. Carefully tip the omelet out onto a warmed plate, folding in half as you go. Repeat to make 3 more omelets.

boiled egg with mustard "soldiers"

Serves **4**
Preparation time **5 minutes**
Cooking time **5 minutes**

2 teaspoons **wholegrain
    mustard**, or to taste
¼ cup **unsalted butter**,
    softened
4 large **eggs**
4 thick slices of **white bread**
black pepper
mustard and cress, to serve

Beat the mustard, butter, and pepper together in a small bowl.

Cook the eggs in a saucepan of boiling water for 4–5 minutes until softly set. Meanwhile, toast the bread, then butter one side with the mustard butter and cut into fingers.

Serve the eggs with the mustard fingers and some mustard and cress.

For boiled egg with asparagus, replace the toasted fingers with freshly steamed asparagus spears. Trim 2 bunches of asparagus spears and peel the stems. Steam or boil for 2 minutes until tender and serve with the boiled egg to dip.

all-in-one veggie breakfast

Serves **4**
Preparation time **10 minutes**
Cooking time **35 minutes**

1 lb **cooked potatoes**, cubed
4 tablespoons **olive oil**
a few **thyme** sprigs
8 oz **button mushrooms**, trimmed
12 **cherry tomatoes**
4 **eggs**
salt and black pepper
2 tablespoons chopped **parsley**, to garnish
buttered toast, to serve (optional)

Spread the potato cubes out in a roasting pan. Drizzle over half the oil, sprinkle with the thyme sprigs, and season with salt and pepper. Bake in a preheated oven, 425°F, for 10 minutes.

Stir the potato cubes well, then add the mushrooms and bake for 10 minutes. Add the tomatoes and bake for an additional 10 minutes.

Make four hollows in between the vegetables and carefully break an egg into each hollow. Bake for 3–4 minutes until the eggs are set. Garnish the vegetable mixture with the parsley and serve straight from the pan, with buttered toast.

For all-in-one veggie supper, without the eggs, use 1 ½ lb potatoes and 12 oz mushrooms. Follow the recipe as above, sprinkling 1 cup grated cheddar cheese over the vegetables for the final 10 minutes of cooking.

cheese, tomato, & basil muffins

Makes **8**
Preparation time **10 minutes**
Cooking time **20–25 minutes**

spray oil, for greasing
1¼ cups **self-rising flour**
½ teaspoon **salt**
⅔ cup **fine cornmeal**
⅔ cup grated **cheddar cheese**
15 pieces drained **sun-dried tomatoes** in oil, chopped
2 tablespoons chopped **basil**
1 **egg**, lightly beaten
1¼ cups **milk**
2 tablespoons **extra virgin olive oil**
butter, to serve

Lightly grease 8 muffin pan holes with spray oil. Sift the flour and salt into a bowl and stir in the cornmeal, ½ cup of the cheese, the tomatoes, and basil. Make a well in the center.

Beat the egg, milk, and oil together in a separate bowl or pitcher, pour into the well and stir together until just combined. The batter should remain a little lumpy.

Divide the batter between the prepared muffin holes and sprinkle with the remaining cheese. Bake in a preheated oven, 350°F, for 20–25 minutes until risen and golden. Allow to cool in the pan for 5 minutes, then transfer to a cooling rack to cool. Serve warm with butter.

For olive & pine nut muffins, replace the sun-dried tomatoes with ½ cup chopped pitted black olives and stir in ½ cup pine nuts. Keep the basil or use chopped fresh thyme instead. Continue the recipe as above.

pesto scrambled eggs

Serves **4**

Preparation time **5 minutes**

Cooking time **5 minutes**

12 **eggs**

6 tablespoons **light cream**

2 tablespoons **butter**

4 slices of **multigrain bread**, toasted

4 tablespoons **Pesto** (see page 86)

salt and black pepper

Beat the eggs, cream, and a little salt and pepper together in a bowl. Melt the butter in a large, nonstick skillet, add the egg mixture and stir over a low heat with a wooden spoon until cooked to your liking.

Put a slice of toast on each serving plate. Spoon a quarter of the scrambled eggs onto each slice of toast, make a small indent in the center and add a tablespoonful of pesto. Serve immediately.

For cheesy scrambled eggs, stir 4 oz diced soft goat cheese and 2 tablespoons chopped parsley into the eggs just before serving, and omit the pesto.

potato rösti with frazzled eggs

Serves **4**
Preparation time **15 minutes**
Cooking time **15 minutes**

1½ lb **round white potatoes**,
  peeled
1 **onion**, thinly sliced
2 teaspoons chopped
  rosemary
4 tablespoons **olive oil**
4 large **eggs**
salt and black pepper
chopped **parsley**, to garnish

Using a box grater, coarsely grate the potatoes. Wrap in a clean dish towel and squeeze out the excess liquid over the sink. Transfer to a bowl and stir in the onion, rosemary, and salt and pepper.

Heat half the oil in a large skillet. Divide the potato mixture into quarters and spoon into 4 x 5 inch mounds in the pan, pressing down to form patties. Cook over a medium heat for 5 minutes on each side, transfer to warmed serving plates, and keep warm in a moderate oven.

Heat the remaining oil in the skillet for about 1 minute until very hot, add the eggs, 2 at a time, and fry until the whites are bubbly and crisp looking. Serve the eggs on the rösti, garnished with chopped parsley.

For rösti with poached eggs, bring a saucepan of lightly salted water to a simmer and add 1 tablespoon white vinegar. Crack an egg into a cup. Swirl the simmering water with a large spoon, gently drop the egg into the center and cook for 2–3 minutes. Carefully remove with a slotted spoon. Repeat with the remaining eggs and finish as above.

mixed mushrooms on toast

Serves **4**
Preparation time **10 minutes**
Cooking time **5 minutes**

2 tablespoons **butter**
3 tablespoons **extra virgin olive oil**, plus extra to serve
1½ lb **mixed mushrooms**, such as oyster, shiitake, flat, and button, trimmed and sliced
2 **garlic cloves**, crushed
1 tablespoon chopped **thyme**
grated zest and juice of 1 **lemon**
2 tablespoons chopped **parsley**
4 slices of **sourdough bread**
2½ cups **mixed salad leaves**
salt and black pepper
fresh **Parmesan cheese shavings**, to serve

Melt the butter with the oil in a large skillet. As soon as the butter stops foaming, add the mushrooms, garlic, thyme, lemon zest, and salt and pepper and cook over a medium heat, stirring, for 4–5 minutes until tender. Sprinkle with the parsley and squeeze over a little lemon juice.

Meanwhile, toast the bread, then arrange it on serving plates.

Top the sourdough toast with an equal quantity of the salad leaves and mushrooms, and drizzle over a little more oil and lemon juice. Sprinkle with Parmesan shavings and serve immediately.

For field mushrooms & Camembert on toast, trim 8 large field mushrooms, brush with 2 tablespoons olive oil and cook under a preheated hot broiler for 4–5 minutes on each side. Lightly toast 4 slices of sourdough bread, top with the mushrooms and arrange 2 slices of Camembert cheese over each one. Cook under the broiler for 2–3 minutes until the cheese has melted then serve.

pancakes with blueberry sauce

Serves **4–6**
Preparation time **10 minutes**
Cooking time **20 minutes**

1 tablespoon **butter**
1¼ cups **self-rising flour**
1 teaspoon **baking soda**
3 tablespoons **superfine sugar**
1 **egg**, beaten
1½ cups **buttermilk**
confectioners' sugar, for dusting
Greek-style yogurt or sour cream, to serve

For the blueberry sauce
1¾ cups fresh **blueberries**
2 tablespoons **honey**
dash of **lemon juice**

Heat the blueberries with the honey and lemon juice in a small saucepan over a low heat for about 3 minutes until they release their juices. Keep warm.

Melt the butter in a separate small saucepan. Sift the flour and baking soda into a bowl and stir in the superfine sugar. Beat the egg and buttermilk together in a separate bowl or pitcher, then gradually beat into the dry ingredients with the melted butter to make a smooth batter.

Heat a nonstick skillet until hot. Drop in large spoonfuls of the batter and cook over a high heat for 3 minutes until bubbles appear on the surface. Flip the pancakes over and cook for an additional minute. Remove and keep warm in a moderate oven. Repeat with the remaining batter.

Serve the pancakes topped with the blueberry sauce and Greek-style yogurt or sour cream, and dusted with confectioners' sugar.

For pancakes with spiced apple sauce, replace the blueberries with 1 peeled, cored, and chopped juicy dessert apple and use maple syrup instead of the honey, adding 1 teaspoon ground cinnamon, or to taste.

honeyed ricotta with summer fruits

Serves **4**

Preparation time **10 minutes**

1 cup fresh **raspberries**

2 teaspoons **rosewater**

1 cup **ricotta cheese**

1⅔ cups fresh **mixed summer berries**

2 tablespoons **honey with honeycomb**

2 tablespoons **pumpkin seeds**, toasted

pinch of ground **cinnamon**

Rub the raspberries through a fine nylon sieve to puree and remove the seeds, then mix with the rosewater. Alternatively, put the raspberries and rosewater in a food processor or blender and process to a puree, then sieve to remove the seeds.

Slice the ricotta into wedges and arrange on serving plates with the berries. Drizzle over the honey and the raspberry puree, adding a little honeycomb, and serve sprinkled with the pumpkin seeds and cinnamon.

For apricot puree to serve with the summer fruits and ricotta, use chopped, pitted, ripe apricots instead of raspberries and orange flower water in place of the rosewater. Puree the apricots in a food processor or blender—there is no need to sieve the puree as it does not contain seeds.

spiced citrus croissants

Serves **2–4**
Preparation time **15 minutes**
Cooking time **5 minutes**

2 **oranges**
3 tablespoons **sour cream**
2 small **ruby or pink grapefruit**
1 teaspoon ground **cinnamon,** plus extra for sprinkling
1 tablespoon **superfine sugar**
4 **croissants**

Grate the zest of one of the oranges and stir into the sour cream in a bowl.

Peel the other orange, then cut the skin and white membrane off both oranges and the grapefruit. Working over a separate bowl to catch the juice, cut between the membranes to remove the segments. Mix the fruit segments and juice with the cinnamon and sugar in a small saucepan. Heat over a low heat for 1–2 minutes.

Meanwhile, put the cròissants on a baking sheet and bake in a preheated oven, 400°F, for 5 minutes, or until thoroughly heated and slightly toasted.

Split the toasted croissants lengthwise and spoon the fruit mixture over the bottom halves. Top with a spoonful of the sour cream mixture and a sprinkling of cinnamon, and replace the top halves. Serve immediately.

For summer strawberry cream croissants, combine 1⅔ cups hulled halved strawberries with ⅔ cup extra thick heavy cream or clotted cream and 1–2 tablespoons confectioners' sugar, to taste. Drizzle over a little elderflower cordial and spoon into toasted croissants.

triple chocolate muffins

Serves **6**
Preparation time **10 minutes**
Cooking time **15 minutes**

⅛ cup **semisweet chocolate chips**
¼ cup **unsalted butter**
2 **eggs**
⅛ cup **superfine sugar**
¾ cup **self-rising flour**
¼ cup **cocoa powder**
2 tablespoons **white chocolate chips**

Line 6 muffin pan holes with paper bake cups.

Melt the semisweet chocolate chips and butter together in a small saucepan over a low heat. Beat the eggs, sugar, flour, and cocoa powder together in a bowl. Fold in the melted chocolate mixture and the white chocolate chips.

Spoon the mixture into the paper bake cups and bake in a preheated oven, 350°F, for 12 minutes until risen and firm to the touch. Transfer to a cooling rack to cool slightly. Serve warm.

For chocolate walnut muffins, replace the white chocolate chips with ⅔ cup roughly chopped walnuts. Continue the recipe as above. Finish the cooked muffins with a teaspoon of melted chocolate on top and a walnut half on each, if you desire.

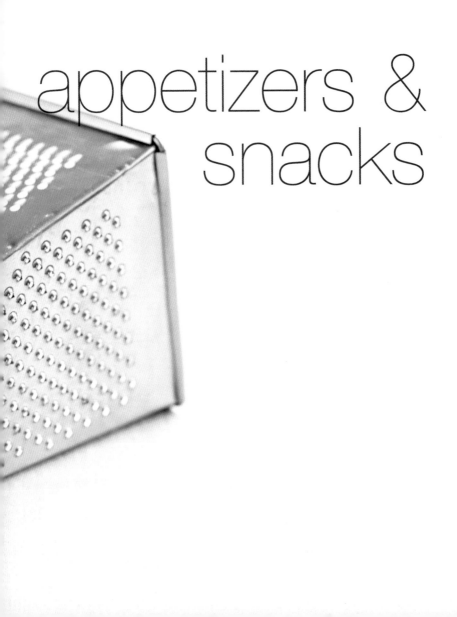

appetizers &
snacks

haloumi with pomegranate salsa

Serves **4**
Preparation time **10 minutes**
Cooking time **5 minutes**

1 lb **haloumi cheese**, sliced
1 tablespoon **honey**

For the pomegranate salsa
½ **pomegranate**
4 tablespoons **extra virgin olive oil**
2 tablespoons chopped **parsley**
1 tablespoon **lemon juice**
1 small **red chili**, seeded and finely chopped
1 small **garlic clove**, crushed
1 teaspoon **pomegranate syrup** (optional)
salt and black pepper

First make the pomegranate salsa. Carefully scoop the pomegranate seeds into a bowl, discarding all the white membrane. Stir in the remaining ingredients and season with salt and pepper.

Heat a large nonstick skillet for 2–3 minutes until hot. Add the haloumi slices, in batches, and cook over a high heat for about 60 seconds on each side until browned and softened.

Meanwhile, warm the honey in a small saucepan until runny.

Transfer the pan-fried haloumi to serving plates and spoon over the salsa. Drizzle the honey over the haloumi and salsa, and serve immediately.

For avocado salsa, peel, pit, and finely dice 1 small ripe avocado and combine with 4 finely chopped scallions, 1 tablespoon lemon juice, 1 tablespoon chopped cilantro, and salt and pepper to taste.

corn & kaffir lime fritters

Serves **4**

Preparation time **20 minutes, plus cooling**

Cooking time **about 45 minutes**

9 oz can **corn kernels**, drained

½ cup **all-purpose flour**

1 teaspoon **baking powder**

1 **egg**, lightly beaten

2 tablespoons **light soy sauce**

1½ tablespoons **lime juice**

4 **Kaffir lime leaves**, very finely shredded

1 tablespoon chopped **cilantro**

2 tablespoons **vegetable oil**

For the chili jam

1 lb ripe **tomatoes**

4 **red bird's eye chilies**

2 **garlic cloves**

2 tablespoons **dark soy sauce**

1 cup **light brown sugar**

5 tablespoons **rice wine vinegar**

½ teaspoon **salt**

First make the chili jam. Roughly chop the tomatoes, chilies, and garlic cloves, then put in a food processor and process until fairly smooth. Transfer to a saucepan and add the remaining ingredients. Bring to a boil, then reduce the heat and simmer gently, stirring occasionally to prevent the sauce sticking, for 30–40 minutes until thick and jam like. Set aside to cool completely.

Put half the corn in a food processor and process until fairly smooth. Sift in the flour and baking powder and add the egg, soy sauce, and lime juice. Process again until combined and transfer to a bowl. Stir in the remaining corn, lime leaves, and cilantro.

Heat the oil in a large skillet. Drop in 6 separate tablespoonfuls of the batter, pat them flat and fry over a medium-high heat for 1½ minutes on each side until cooked through. Repeat with the remaining batter to make 12 x 2 inch fritters. Serve the fritters hot with the chili jam, garnished with lime wedges and cilantro sprigs.

For corn fritter wraps, serve the fritters in lettuce cups, using 4 large iceberg or romaine lettuce leaves. Add the chili jam, wrap and serve. For a more substantial wrap, use wheat tortillas to wrap the fritters with shredded lettuce and the chili jam.

gnocchi with sage butter

Serves **4**
Preparation time **30 minutes**
Cooking time **15–18 minutes**

1 lb **floury potatoes**, cubed
1 **egg**, beaten
1 teaspoon **sea salt**
2 tablespoons **olive oil**
1½ cups **all-purpose flour**
½ cup **butter**
2 tablespoons chopped **sage**
salt
freshly grated **Parmesan cheese**, to serve

Cook the potatoes in a saucepan of lightly salted boiling water for 10–12 minutes until tender. Drain, return the potatoes to the pan and heat gently for several seconds to dry out. Mash the potatoes and beat in the egg, salt, oil, and flour to form a sticky dough.

Take walnut-size pieces of the dough and roll into egg shapes, rolling them over the tines of a fork.

Bring a large saucepan of lightly salted water to a rolling boil, add half the gnocchi (freeze the remainder for later use) and cook for 3 minutes until they rise to the surface. Drain the gnocchi and transfer to serving bowls.

Meanwhile, melt the butter in a skillet. As soon as it stops foaming, add the sage and fry over a medium-high heat, stirring, for 2–3 minutes until crisp and the butter turns golden brown. Drizzle over the gnocchi, sprinkle with grated Parmesan, and serve immediately.

For gnocchi, plum tomato, & sage butter gratin, follow the recipe above, but once the gnocchi is drained, spoon it into 4 individual gratin dishes and divide 8 quartered plum tomatoes equally between the dishes. Mix the tomatoes in with the gnocchi. Pour the sage butter over the gnocchi and sprinkle with grated Parmesan. Brown under a preheated hot broiler for 1–2 minutes until golden.

sweet potato & fontina panini

Serves **2–4**
Preparation time **10 minutes**
Cooking time **10–15 minutes**

8 oz **sweet potato**, peeled
  and thinly sliced
1 tablespoon **extra virgin
  olive oil**
vegetable oil, for pan-frying
12 **sage leaves**
1 **ciabatta**
2 tablespoons ready-made
  olive tapenade
8 oz **fontina cheese**, thinly
  sliced
salt and black pepper

Brush the sweet potato slices with the olive oil and season lightly with salt and pepper. Heat a ridged griddle pan until hot. Add the sweet potato slices, in batches if necessary, and cook for 3–4 minutes on each side until charred and tender. Remove and set aside. Clean the griddle pan.

Meanwhile, heat a little vegetable oil in a small skillet, add the sage leaves and fry over a medium-high heat, stirring, for 1–2 minutes until crisp. Remove and drain on paper towels.

Cut the ciabatta into quarters, then trim the quarters so that all 4 pieces will fit in the griddle pan. Heat the griddle pan and brush with a little vegetable oil. Add the ciabatta pieces, cut-side down, and cook for 1 minute, or until toasted and charred. Depending on the size of your griddle pan, you may have to toast the bread in 2 batches.

Spread the toasted sides of the ciabatta with the tapenade and sandwich together with layers of fontina, sage leaves, and sweet potato slices.

Add the whole sandwiches to the griddle pan and cook for 1–2 minutes on each side until toasted and the cheese in the center has melted. Serve immediately with a green salad.

For eggplant & mozzarella panini, use 1 large eggplant, sliced widthwise into ¼ inch slices, instead of the sweet potato, and replace the fontina with mozzarella. Flavor with basil leaves, unfried, instead of sage. Continue the recipe as above.

bruschetta with tomatoes & ricotta

Serves **4**

Preparation time **10 minutes**

Cooking time **15 minutes**

1 lb **vine-ripened cherry tomatoes**

2 tablespoons **extra virgin olive oil**

4 large slices of **sourdough bread**

1 large **garlic clove**, peeled

1½ cups **ricotta cheese**

½ quantity **Basil Oil** (see page 124)

salt and black pepper

basil leaves, to garnish

Spread the tomatoes out in a roasting pan, season with salt and pepper and drizzle with the extra virgin olive oil. Roast in a preheated oven, 425°F, for 15 minutes.

Meanwhile, heat a ridged griddle pan until hot. Add the bread slices and cook until toasted and charred on both sides. Rub all over with the garlic clove.

Top each bruschetta with a slice of ricotta and the roasted tomatoes, and drizzle over the basil oil. Garnish with basil leaves.

For bruschetta with fig, arugula, & feta, toast 4 slices of sourdough bread as in the recipe above and rub each slice with garlic. Combine 4 quartered fresh figs with 5 oz crumbled feta cheese, a good handful of baby arugula leaves, and some chopped mint. Arrange on the bruschetta and serve drizzled with extra virgin olive oil.

crostini with pea & ricotta pesto

Serves **6**

Preparation time **10 minutes**, plus cooling

Cooking time **10 minutes**

1 small **French stick**, sliced

3 tablespoons **extra virgin olive oil**, plus extra to serve

1⅔ cups fresh or frozen shelled **peas**

1 small **garlic clove**, crushed

3 tablespoons **ricotta cheese**

juice of ½ lemon

1 tablespoon chopped **mint**

2½ tablespoons freshly grated **Parmesan cheese**

salt and black pepper

Lay the bread slices on a baking sheet, brush lightly with 1 tablespoon of the oil and bake in a preheated oven, 375°F, for 5–6 minutes until crisp and golden. Allow to cool on a cooling rack while you prepare the pesto.

Cook the peas in a saucepan of lightly salted boiling water for 3 minutes. Drain and immediately refresh under cold water. Put the peas in a food processor, add the remaining oil, the garlic, ricotta, lemon juice, mint, Parmesan, and salt and pepper and process until fairly smooth.

Spread the crostini with the pesto and serve drizzled with oil.

For fava bean & dill pesto, replace the peas with 1½ cups frozen (or fresh shelled) fava beans and cook in a saucepan of lightly salted boiling water for 3 minutes. Drain well, refresh under cold water and continue as in the recipe above, replacing the mint with an equal amount of chopped dill.

sage & goat cheese frittata

Serves **4**
Preparation time **10 minutes**
Cooking time **10 minutes**

2 tablespoons **butter**, plus
    extra if necessary
18 large **sage leaves**
2 oz **soft goat cheese**,
    crumbled
2 tablespoons **sour cream**
4 **eggs**
salt and black pepper

Melt the butter in a nonstick skillet. As soon as it stops foaming, add the sage leaves and fry over a medium-high heat, stirring, for 2–3 minutes until crisp and the butter turns golden brown. Take out 6 of the leaves and drain on paper towels. Transfer the remaining leaves and butter to a bowl.

Beat the goat cheese and sour cream together in a separate bowl. Beat the eggs in another bowl, season with salt and pepper, then stir in the sage leaves with the butter.

Reheat the skillet, adding a little extra butter if necessary. Pour in the egg mixture and dot over spoonfuls of the goat cheese mixture. Cook over a medium heat for 4–5 minutes until the underside is set, then transfer to a preheated hot broiler to brown the top lightly. Allow to cool slightly, then gently slide the frittata onto a serving plate. Garnish with the reserved sage leaves and serve with crusty bread.

For spinach & goat cheese frittata, cook 3½ cups baby spinach leaves and 1 crushed garlic clove in the butter instead of the sage leaves for 2 minutes, or until the spinach has wilted. Stir into the beaten eggs at the second stage and continue with the recipe as above.

baked figs with goat cheese

Serves **4**
Preparation time **10 minutes**
Cooking time **10–12 minutes**

8 firm but ripe fresh **figs**
3 oz **soft goat cheese**
8 **mint leaves**
2 tablespoons **extra virgin olive oil**
salt and black pepper

For the arugula salad
3 cups **baby arugula leaves**
1 tablespoon **extra virgin olive oil**
1 teaspoon **lemon juice**
salt and black pepper

Cut a cross in the top of each fig without cutting through the base. Put 1 teaspoonful of the goat cheese and a mint leaf in each fig. Transfer to a roasting pan, then season with salt and pepper and drizzle with the oil. Bake in a preheated oven, 375°F, for 10–12 minutes until the figs are soft and the cheese has melted.

Put the baby arugula leaves in a bowl. Beat together the oil, lemon juice, salt, and pepper and drizzle over the leaves. Serve with the figs.

For figs stuffed with mozzarella & basil, replace the goat cheese with 4 oz sliced mozzarella and use basil leaves instead of the mint leaves. Continue the recipe as above. Serve with sprigs of watercress instead of the arugula salad.

tofu with chili vinegar dressing

Serves **4**

Preparation time **15 minutes**, plus cooling

Cooking time **about 15 minutes**

vegetable oil, for deep-frying

2 cups **silken tofu**, drained

⅓ cup **cornstarch**

2 teaspoons **salt**, plus extra to serve

1 teaspoon **Chinese five-spice powder**, plus extra to serve

For the chili vinegar dressing

5 tablespoons **rice wine vinegar**

5 tablespoons **water**

2 tablespoons **superfine sugar**

1 tablespoon **light soy sauce**

1 large **red chili**, seeded and finely chopped

1 teaspoon **sesame oil**

First make the dressing. Combine the vinegar, measurement water, and sugar in a bowl and stir until the sugar has dissolved. Bring to a boil in a saucepan, then reduce the heat and simmer for 5–6 minutes until reduced by half and syrup-like. Allow to cool for 30 minutes, then stir in the soy sauce, chili, and sesame oil. Pour into a serving bowl.

Heat 2 inches vegetable oil in a deep, heavy saucepan until it reaches 350–375°F, or until a cube of bread browns in 30 seconds. Meanwhile, cut the tofu into 1¼ inch cubes. Combine the cornstarch, salt, and Chinese five-spice powder in a bowl. Dip the tofu cubes, a few pieces at a time, in the cornstarch mixture, add to the hot oil and deep-fry for 2–3 minutes until crisp and golden. Remove with a slotted spoon and drain on paper towels.

Arrange the tofu on a serving platter and dust with a little extra salt and Chinese five-spice powder. Serve with the chili vinegar dressing for dipping.

For roasted spiced tofu, cut 1 lb firm tofu into 1 inch cubes. Combine with 2 tablespoons soy sauce, 1 tablespoon sweet chili sauce, 1 teaspoon honey, and a pinch of Chinese five-spice powder. Spread out in a roasting pan and roast in a preheated oven, 425°F, for 15–20 minutes until golden.

eggplant dip with flatbreads

Serves **6**

Preparation time **15 minutes**,
   plus cooling

Cooking time **15 minutes**

1 large **eggplant**

4 tablespoons **extra virgin
   olive oil**

1 teaspoon ground **cumin**

⅔ cup **Greek-style or whole
   milk yogurt**

1 small **garlic clove**, crushed

2 tablespoons chopped
   cilantro

1 tablespoon **lemon juice**

4 **flour tortillas**

salt and black pepper

Cut the eggplant lengthwise into ¼ inch thick slices.
Mix 3 tablespoons of the oil with the cumin and salt
and pepper and brush all over the eggplant slices.
Cook in a preheated ridged griddle pan or under a
preheated hot broiler for 3–4 minutes on each side
until charred and tender. Allow to cool, then finely chop.

Mix the eggplant into the yogurt in a bowl, then stir in
the garlic, cilantro, lemon juice, the remaining oil, and
salt and pepper to taste. Transfer to a serving bowl.

Cook the tortillas in the preheated griddle pan or
under the preheated hot broiler for 3 minutes on
each side until toasted. Cut into triangles and serve
immediately with the eggplant dip.

For cucumber & mint dip, finely grate ½ cucumber
and squeeze dry, then put in a bowl and stir in the
remaining dip ingredients as above, replacing the
cilantro with an equal amount of chopped mint.

felafel pita pockets

Serves **4**

Preparation time **15 minutes**, plus soaking

Cooking time **12 minutes**

1½ cups **dried chickpeas**

1 small **onion**, finely chopped

2 **garlic cloves**, crushed

½ bunch **parsley**

½ bunch **cilantro**

2 teaspoons **ground coriander**

½ teaspoon **baking powder**

vegetable oil, for pan-frying

4 **pita breads**

handful of **salad leaves**

2 **tomatoes**, diced

Greek-style or whole milk yogurt, to serve

Put the dried chickpeas in a bowl, add cold water to cover by a generous 4 inches and allow to soak overnight.

Drain the chickpeas, transfer to a food processor and process until coarsely ground. Add the onion, garlic, herbs, ground coriander, baking powder, and salt and pepper and process until really smooth. Using wet hands, shape the mixture into 16 small patties.

Heat a little vegetable oil in a large skillet, add the patties, in batches, and fry over a medium-high heat for 3 minutes on each side until golden and cooked through. Remove and drain on paper towels.

Split the pita breads and fill with the felafel, salad leaves, and diced tomatoes. Add a spoonful of Greek-style or whole milk yogurt and serve immediately.

For felafel salad, toss 4 handfuls of mixed salad leaves with a little extra virgin olive oil, lemon juice, and salt and pepper, and arrange on serving plates. Core, seed, and dice 1 red bell pepper and sprinkle it over the salads. Top with the felafel and spoon over a little Tahini Yogurt Sauce (see page 76).

pumpkin with walnut pesto

Serves **4**
Preparation time **15 minutes**
Cooking time **20–25 minutes**

2 lb **pumpkin**
extra virgin olive oil, for
  brushing
salt and black pepper

For the walnut pesto
½ cup **walnuts**, toasted
2 **scallions**, trimmed and
  chopped
1 large **garlic clove**, crushed
1¼ cups **arugula leaves**, plus
  extra to serve
3 tablespoons **walnut oil**
3 tablespoons **extra virgin**
  olive oil

Cut the pumpkin into 8 wedges. Remove the seeds and fiber but leave the skin on. Brush all over with olive oil, season with salt and pepper, and spread out on a large baking sheet. Roast in a preheated oven, 425°F, for 20–25 minutes until tender, turning halfway through.

Meanwhile, make the pesto. Put the walnuts, scallions, garlic, and arugula in a food processor and process until finely chopped. With the motor running, gradually drizzle in the oils. Season the pesto with salt and pepper.

Serve the roasted pumpkin with the pesto and extra arugula leaves.

For gnocchi with walnut pesto, make the pesto as in the recipe above. Prepare and cook the gnocchi following the recipe on page 46, using half the amount for an appetizer or all the gnocchi for a main course. If you already have a half quantity of gnocchi in the freezer, cook it from frozen in a large saucepan of lightly salted boiling water for 5–6 minutes until the gnocchi rise to the surface, then drain, transfer to a buttered serving dish, and top with the pesto.

mushroom & ginger wontons

Serves **4**
Preparation time **30 minutes**,
  plus cooling
Cooking time **10–12 minutes**

2 tablespoons **vegetable oil**
1 **garlic clove**, crushed
1 teaspoon grated **fresh
  ginger root**
8 oz **mixed mushrooms**,
  trimmed and finely chopped
1 tablespoon **dark soy sauce**
1 tablespoon chopped
  cilantro
16 **wonton skins**

**For the Szechuan chili
  dressing**
1 teaspoon **dried red pepper
  flakes**
⅔ cup **vegetable stock**
1 tablespoon **rice wine
  vinegar**
1 tablespoon **light soy sauce**
2 teaspoons **superfine sugar**
¼ teaspoon freshly ground
  Szechuan pepper

Heat the oil in a skillet, add the garlic and ginger and cook over a medium heat, stirring, for 2–3 minutes. Add the mushrooms and soy sauce and cook, stirring, for 3–4 minutes until golden. Remove from the heat, season with salt and pepper and stir in the cilantro. Allow to cool.

Meanwhile, make the dressing. Put all the ingredients in a saucepan and heat over a low heat, stirring, until hot but not boiling. Keep warm.

Put a teaspoon of the mushroom mixture in the center of each wonton skin. Brush a little water around the filling and fold the wontons in half diagonally, pressing the edges together to seal.

Bring a large saucepan of lightly salted water to a rolling boil, add the wontons and cook for 2–3 minutes until they rise to the surface. Gently drain and transfer to warmed serving bowls. Strain over the dressing and serve immediately.

For crispy mushroom wontons, heat 2 inches vegetable oil in a wok or deep, heavy saucepan until it reaches 350–375°F, or until a cube of bread browns in 30 seconds. Add the wontons, in batches, and deep-fry for 2–3 minutes until crisp and golden. Remove with a slotted spoon and drain on paper towels. Serve with Chili Jam (see page 44). Wonton skins are available fresh or frozen from Asian markets.

bean, lemon, & rosemary hummus

Serves **4–6**
Preparation time **10 minutes**,
  plus cooling
Cooking time **10 minutes**

6 tablespoons **extra virgin
  olive oil**, plus extra to serve
4 **shallots**, finely chopped
2 large **garlic cloves**, crushed
1 teaspoon chopped
  rosemary, plus extra sprigs
  to garnish
grated zest and juice of
  ½ **lemon**
2 x 13 oz cans **lima beans**
salt and black pepper
toasted ciabatta, to serve

Heat the oil in a skillet, add the shallots, garlic, chopped rosemary, and lemon zest and cook over a low heat, stirring occasionally, for 10 minutes until the shallots are softened. Allow to cool.

Transfer the shallot mixture to a food processor, add all the remaining ingredients and process until smooth.

Spread the hummus onto toasted ciabatta, garnish with rosemary sprigs and serve drizzled with oil.

For chickpea & chili hummus, put 2 x 13 oz cans drained chickpeas in a food processor with 2 seeded and chopped red chilies, 1 large crushed garlic clove, 2 tablespoons lemon juice, and salt and pepper to taste. Process with enough extra virgin olive oil to form a soft paste. Serve as a dip with vegetable crudités.

onion, walnut, & blue cheese tarts

Makes **8**

Preparation time **20 minutes**,
plus cooling

Cooking time **35–40 minutes**

3 tablespoons **butter**

1 lb **onions**, thinly sliced

2 **garlic cloves**, crushed

1 tablespoon chopped **thyme**

½ cup **walnuts**, chopped

11½ oz **puff pastry**, defrosted
if frozen

all-purpose flour, for dusting

5 oz **blue cheese**, diced

Melt the butter in a skillet, add the onions, garlic, and thyme and cook over a medium heat, stirring occasionally, for 20–25 minutes until soft and golden. Stir in the walnuts. Allow to cool.

Roll the pastry out on a lightly floured work surface to form a rectangle 16 x 8 inches, trimming the edges. Cut the rectangle vertically in half, then cut horizontally into quarters to make eight 4 inch squares.

Divide the onion mixture between the squares, spreading over the surface but leaving a narrow border around the edges. Sprinkle with the blue cheese. Transfer the pastries to a large baking sheet and bake in a preheated oven, 425°F, for 12–15 minutes until the pastry is puffed and the cheese is golden. Allow to cool slightly and serve warm.

For onion & goat cheese tart, roll the pastry out but leave whole and lay on a baking sheet. Spread the onion mixture over the pastry, leaving a ½ inch border. Sprinkle with 7 oz crumbled or diced soft goat cheese and bake for 20–25 minutes until the pastry is puffed up and the cheese is golden.

main
meals

butternut squash, tofu, & pea curry

Serves **4**
Preparation time **15 minutes**
Cooking time **25 minutes**

1 tablespoon **sunflower oil**
1 tablespoon **Thai red curry paste**
1 lb peeled, seeded **butternut squash**, cubed
2 cups **vegetable stock**
13 oz can **coconut milk**
6 Kaffir **lime leaves**, bruised, plus extra shredded leaves to garnish
1⅓ cups **frozen peas**
1⅔ cups diced **firm tofu**
2 tablespoons **light soy sauce**
juice of 1 **lime**
chopped **cilantro**, to garnish
finely chopped **red chili**, to garnish

Heat the oil in a wok or deep skillet, add the curry paste and stir-fry over a low heat for 1 minute. Add the squash, stir-fry briefly and then add the stock, coconut milk, and the bruised lime leaves. Bring to a boil, then cover, reduce the heat and simmer gently for 15 minutes until the squash is cooked.

Stir in the peas, tofu, soy sauce, and lime juice and simmer for an additional 5 minutes until the peas are cooked. Spoon into serving bowls, garnish with shredded lime leaves and chopped cilantro.

For green vegetable curry, use green curry paste instead of red curry paste. Replace the squash with 1 sliced carrot, 1 sliced zucchini, and 1 cored, seeded, and sliced red bell pepper and continue as in the recipe above.

broiled vegetables & couscous

Serves **4**
Preparation time **20 minutes**
Cooking time **16–20 minutes**

1 large **eggplant**
2 large **zucchini**
2 **red bell peppers**, cored,
   seeded, and quartered
4 tablespoons **olive oil**
1 cup **couscous**
2 cups boiling **vegetable
   stock**
¼ cup **butter**
2 tablespoons chopped
   mixed herbs, such as mint,
   cilantro, and parsley
juice of 1 **lemon**
salt and black pepper

For the tahini yogurt sauce
½ cup **Greek-style or whole
   milk yogurt**
1 tablespoon **tahini paste**
   (see page 13)
1 **garlic clove**, crushed
½ tablespoon **lemon juice**
1 tablespoon **extra virgin
   olive oil**

Cut the eggplant and zucchini into ¼ inch thick slices
and put in a large bowl with the bell peppers. Add the
olive oil and salt and pepper and stir well.

Heat a ridged griddle pan until hot. Add the vegetables,
in batches, and cook for 3–4 minutes on each side,
depending on size, until charred and tender.

Meanwhile, prepare the couscous. Put the couscous
in a heatproof bowl. Pour over the boiling stock, cover
and allow to soak for 5 minutes. Fluff up the grains
with a fork and stir in the butter, herbs, lemon juice,
and salt and pepper to taste.

Make the tahini yogurt sauce. Combine all the
ingredients in a bowl and season with salt and pepper.
Serve with the vegetables and couscous.

For garlic mayonnaise to serve instead of the tahini
yogurt sauce, crush 1–2 garlic cloves and stir into
⅔ cup good-quality mayonnaise. Serve with the
vegetables and couscous.

roasted stuffed peppers

Serves **2**
Preparation time **10 minutes**
Cooking time **55 minutes–
    1 hour**

4 large **red bell peppers**
2 **garlic cloves**, crushed
1 tablespoon chopped **thyme**,
    plus extra to garnish
4 **plum tomatoes**, halved
4 tablespoons **extra virgin
    olive oil**
2 tablespoons **balsamic
    vinegar**
salt and black pepper

Cut the red bell peppers in half lengthwise, then scoop out and discard the cores and seeds. Put the pepper halves, cut-sides up, in a roasting pan lined with foil or a ceramic dish. Divide the garlic and thyme between them and season with salt and pepper.

Put a tomato half in each pepper and drizzle with the oil and vinegar. Roast in a preheated oven, 425°F, for 55 minutes–1 hour until the peppers are soft and charred.

Serve with some crusty bread to mop up the juices and a baby leaf salad, if you desire.

For colorful, cheesy roasted peppers, use a mixture of green, yellow, and red bell peppers. After 45 minutes cooking time, top each pepper with a slice of mozzarella cheese and return to the oven for the remaining 10–15 minutes. Serve with wedges of whole-wheat soda bread.

creamy pea & mint risotto with brie

Serves **4**
Preparation time **15 minutes**
Cooking time **35 minutes**

5 cups **vegetable stock**
¼ cup **butter**
1 large **onion**, finely chopped
2 **garlic cloves**, crushed
1½ cups **arborio rice**
⅔ cup **dry white wine**
2⅓ cups fresh or frozen
   shelled **peas**
½ bunch fresh **mint leaves,**
   torn
2 oz **Brie**, diced
salt and black pepper
freshly grated **Parmesan**
   cheese, to serve

Put the stock in a saucepan and bring to a very gentle simmer.

Meanwhile, melt the butter in a saucepan, add the onion, garlic, and salt and pepper and cook over a low heat, stirring occasionally, for 10 minutes until the onion is softened but not browned. Add the rice and cook, stirring, for 1 minute until all the grains are glossy. Stir in the wine, bring to a boil, and continue to boil for 1–2 minutes until absorbed. Stir in the peas.

Stir about ⅔ cup of the stock into the rice. Cook over a medium heat, stirring constantly, until absorbed. Continue to add the stock, a little at a time, and cook, stirring constantly, for about 20 minutes until the rice is al dente and the stock has all been absorbed.

Remove the pan from the heat. Stir in the mint and Brie, cover, and allow to stand for 5 minutes until the cheese has melted. Serve with grated Parmesan.

For rice patties, leave the risotto until completely cold, then stir in 1 beaten egg. Divide the mixture into small patties and coat with dried bread crumbs. Heat a little vegetable oil in a skillet, add the patties and fry for 2–3 minutes on each side until golden and cooked through. Serve with a green salad.

fava bean & lemon spaghetti

Serves **4**
Preparation time **10 minutes**
Cooking time **15–18 minutes**

1 lb **dried spaghetti**
2 cups fresh or frozen shelled
  fava beans
4 tablespoons **extra virgin**
  olive oil
3 **garlic cloves**, finely
  chopped
pinch of **dried red pepper**
  flakes
grated zest and juice of
  1 **lemon**
2 tablespoons torn **basil**
  leaves
salt and black pepper
freshly grated **Parmesan or**
  pecorino cheese, to serve
  (optional)

Cook the pasta in a large saucepan of lightly salted boiling water for 10–12 minutes, or according to the package instructions, until al dente. Drain, reserving 4 tablespoons of the cooking water, and return the pasta to the pan.

Meanwhile, cook the beans in a separate saucepan of salted boiling water for 3–4 minutes. Drain well.

While the pasta and beans are cooking, heat the oil in a skillet, add the garlic, pepper flakes, lemon zest, and salt and pepper and cook over a low heat, stirring, for 3–4 minutes until the garlic is soft but not browned.

Scrape the oil mixture into the pasta with the beans, reserved pasta cooking water, lemon juice, and basil and stir over a medium heat until heated through. Serve with grated Parmesan or pecorino.

For spaghetti with peas & mint, replace the fava beans with 2½ cups shelled fresh peas and cook as in the recipe above, adding 2 tablespoons chopped mint instead of the basil just before serving. Frozen petit pois can be used instead of fresh peas.

leek & thyme sausages with relish

Serves **4**
Preparation time **25 minutes**,
   plus soaking and cooling
Cooking time **45–50 minutes**

1 tablespoon **olive oil**
1 **leek**, trimmed and finely
   chopped
2 teaspoons chopped **thyme**
1⅓ cups grated **cheddar**
   cheese
3 cups **fresh whole-wheat**
   bread crumbs
⅓ cup **ricotta cheese**
1 tablespoon **wholegrain**
   mustard
1 **egg**, beaten
½ cup **dried white or whole-**
   wheat bread crumbs
sunflower oil, for pan-frying
salt and black pepper

For the relish
2 tablespoons **olive oil**
2 **red onions**, thinly sliced
½ cup **dried cranberries**
1 tablespoon **balsamic**
   vinegar
½ cup **cranberry sauce**

First make the relish. Heat the olive oil in a saucepan, add the onions and cook over a medium heat, stirring occasionally, for 20–25 minutes until soft and golden. Meanwhile, soak the cranberries in the vinegar. Add to the onions with the cranberry sauce and 2 tablespoons water and cook for 10 minutes until thickened and jam-like. Season with salt and pepper and allow to cool.

Meanwhile, heat the olive oil in a skillet, add the leek and thyme and cook over a medium heat, stirring frequently, for 5 minutes. Allow to cool.

Combine the leek mixture, cheddar, fresh bread crumbs, ricotta, mustard, and salt and pepper in a bowl. Stir in the egg and mix together to form a soft dough. Shape into 12 sausages and roll each one in the dried bread crumbs.

Heat a little sunflower oil in a skillet, add the sausages and fry over a medium heat, turning frequently, for 10 minutes until golden and cooked through. Serve immediately with the relish.

For leek & thyme burgers with blue cheese, use finely crumbled Danish blue cheese instead of the cheddar. Shape the sausage mixture into 8 patties, coat in dried bread crumbs, and pan-fry as above. Serve in soft bread rolls with shredded lettuce and sliced tomatoes.

eggplant toasties with pesto

Serves **4**
Preparation time **15 minutes**
Cooking time **8–20 minutes**

1 large **eggplant**
4 tablespoons **extra virgin olive oil**
4 slices **sourdough bread**
2 **beefsteak tomatoes**, thickly sliced
7 oz **mozzarella cheese**, sliced
salt and black pepper

For the pesto
1¼ cups **basil leaves**
1 **garlic clove**, crushed
4 tablespoons **pine nuts**
6 tablespoons **extra virgin olive oil**
2 tablespoons freshly grated **Parmesan cheese**

First make the pesto. Put the basil, garlic, pine nuts, oil, and salt and pepper in a food processor and process until fairly smooth. Transfer to a bowl, stir in the Parmesan and adjust the seasoning. Set aside until required.

Cut the eggplant into ½ inch thick slices. Season the oil with salt and pepper and brush over the eggplant slices. Heat a ridged griddle pan until hot. Add the eggplant slices, in batches if necessary, and cook for 4–5 minutes on each side until charred and tender.

Meanwhile, broil the sourdough bread.

Top the broiled bread with an eggplant slice. Spread with the pesto. Top with tomato and mozzarella slices and more pesto. Cook under a preheated hot broiler for 1–2 minutes until bubbling and golden.

For eggplant buck rarebit, arrange the eggplant slices on large toasted soft bread roll halves with the pesto, sliced tomatoes, and mozzarella. Broil until brown. Top each with a poached egg and serve immediately.

beet & goat cheese risotto

Serves **4–6**
Preparation time **15 minutes**
Cooking time **35 minutes**

5 cups **vegetable stock**
1½ cups diced **cooked beets**
4 tablespoons **extra virgin olive oil**
1 **red onion**, finely chopped
2 **garlic cloves**, crushed
2 teaspoons chopped **thyme**, plus extra to garnish
1½ cups **arborio rice**
½ cup **red wine**
4 oz **soft goat cheese**, diced
1 cup **pecan nuts**, toasted and chopped
salt and black pepper

Put the stock and any beet juices in a saucepan and bring to a very gentle simmer.

Meanwhile, heat the oil in a separate saucepan, add the onion, garlic, thyme, and salt and pepper and cook over a low heat, stirring occasionally, for 10 minutes until the onion is softened but not browned. Add the rice and cook, stirring, for 1 minute until all the grains are glossy. Stir in the wine, bring to a boil and continue to boil for 1–2 minutes until absorbed. Stir in the beet.

Stir about ⅔ cup of the stock into the rice. Cook over a medium heat, stirring constantly, until absorbed. Continue to add the stock, a little at a time, and cook, stirring constantly, for about 20 minutes until the rice is al dente and the stock has all been absorbed.

Remove the pan from the heat. Stir in the goat cheese and pecan nuts, cover, and allow to stand for 2–3 minutes until the cheese has melted. Serve with an arugula salad.

For beet & mascarpone risotto with pine nuts,
replace the goat cheese with 5 oz mascarpone cheese. Sprinkle the risotto with pine nuts (about 1 tablespoon per portion) instead of adding pecan nuts. Vacuum-packed cooked beet is available from most supermarkets and is the best type (other than freshly cooked) to use for this recipe.

spinach & mushroom lasagna

Serves **6–8**

Preparation time **35 minutes**,
  plus infusing

Cooking time **45–50 minutes**

4 tablespoons **olive oil**

2 **garlic cloves**, crushed

2 teaspoons chopped **thyme**

1 lb **button mushrooms**,
  trimmed and sliced

2½ cups frozen **leaf spinach**,
  defrosted

spray oil, for greasing

7 oz fresh **lasagna sheets**

salt and black pepper

For the cheese sauce

5 cups **milk**

2 fresh **bay leaves**

¼ cup **unsalted butter**, plus
  extra for greasing

½ cup **all-purpose flour**

2 cups grated **cheddar
  cheese**

First make the sauce. Put the milk and bay leaves in a saucepan and heat to boiling point. Remove from the heat and allow to infuse for 20 minutes. Discard the bay leaves.

Melt the butter in a separate saucepan, add the flour and cook over a medium heat, stirring constantly, for 1 minute. Gradually stir in the milk and continue to cook, stirring, until the mixture boils. Reduce the heat and simmer for 2 minutes. Remove from the heat, add most of the cheddar, and stir until melted.

Meanwhile, heat the oil in a skillet, add the garlic, thyme, mushrooms, and salt and pepper and cook over a medium heat, stirring frequently, for 5 minutes until tender. Squeeze out the excess water from the spinach and roughly chop. Stir into the mushroom mixture. Remove from the heat.

Lightly grease a 5 cup lasagna dish with spray oil. Spread a quarter of the cheese sauce over the base and add one-third of the mushroom and spinach mixture and a lasagna sheet. Repeat these layers twice more. Add a final layer of sauce to cover the lasagna and sprinkle with the remaining cheese. Bake in a preheated oven, 375°F, for 35–40 minutes until browned.

For mushroom, flageolet, & tomato lasagna, replace the spinach with a tomato sauce (see page 186). Add a drained 14 oz can flageolet beans to the mushroom mixture and layer with the tomato sauce, lasagna sheets, and cheese sauce, and bake as the above recipe.

90

omelet with basil tomatoes

Serves **4**
Preparation time **10 minutes**
Cooking time **16–20 minutes**

4 tablespoons **extra virgin
    olive oil**
1 lb **cherry tomatoes**, halved
a few chopped **basil leaves**
12 **eggs**
2 tablespoons **wholegrain
    mustard**
¼ cup **butter**
4 oz **soft goat cheese**, diced
salt and black pepper
watercress, to garnish

Heat the oil in a large skillet, add the tomatoes, in batches if necessary, and cook, stirring gently, for 2–3 minutes until softened. Add the basil and season with salt and pepper. Transfer to a bowl and keep warm in a moderate oven.

Beat the eggs, mustard, and salt and pepper together in a separate bowl. Melt a quarter of the butter in an omelet pan or small skillet. As soon as it stops foaming, swirl in a quarter of the egg mixture and cook over a medium heat, forking over the omelet so that it cooks evenly.

Dot a quarter of the goat cheese over one half of the omelet as soon as it is set on the underside, but still a little runny in the center, and cook for an additional 30 seconds. Carefully slide the omelet on to a warmed serving plate, folding it in half as you go. Keep warm in the oven. Repeat with the remaining egg mixture to make 3 more omelets.

Garnish the omelets with watercress and serve with the tomatoes and a green salad.

For tomato stuffed omelet, omit the first step of the above recipe. Arrange a quarter of the tomatoes with the goat cheese over one half of the omelet as soon as it is set on the underside. Follow the recipe above to finish the omelet and then serve with an arugula salad.

vegetable kebabs with pilaf

Serves **4**

Preparation time **20 minutes**,
  plus marinating and standing

Cooking time **25 minutes**

1 tablespoon chopped
  rosemary

5 tablespoons **extra virgin
  olive oil**

2 **zucchini**

1 large **red bell pepper**, cored
  and seeded

16 **button mushrooms**,
  trimmed

8 **cherry tomatoes**

**Greek-style or whole milk
  yogurt**, to serve

For the pilaf

1¼ cups **basmati rice**

1 **onion**, finely chopped

2 **garlic cloves**, finely
  chopped

6 **cardamom pods**, bruised

1 cup **dried cranberries**

½ cup **pistachio nuts**, toasted
  and chopped

2 tablespoons chopped
  cilantro

salt and black pepper

Combine the rosemary with 2 tablespoons of the oil and salt and pepper in a large bowl. Cut the zucchini and bell pepper into large pieces, add to the oil with the mushrooms and tomatoes, and toss well. Cover and allow to marinate for 20 minutes.

Wash the rice under cold water, drain, and put in a saucepan. Add lightly salted water to cover the rice by at least 2 inches. Bring to a boil and boil for 10 minutes. Drain well.

Heat the remaining oil in a separate saucepan, add the onion, garlic, and cardamom pods and cook over a medium heat, stirring frequently, for 5 minutes until lightly golden. Add the rice, cranberries, pistachio nuts, cilantro, and salt and pepper. Stir well, then remove from the heat, cover, and allow to stand for 10 minutes.

Meanwhile, heat a ridged griddle pan until hot. Thread the vegetables alternately onto 8 wooden skewers, presoaked in cold water for 30 minutes. Add to the pan and cook, turning frequently, for 10 minutes until all the vegetables are tender. Serve with the rice and Greek-style or whole milk yogurt.

For mixed spice pilaf, boil the rice as above, adding ¼ teaspoon saffron threads to the water. Cook 1 chopped onion, 2 crushed garlic cloves, 1 cinnamon stick, and 6 whole cloves in ¼ cup butter for 5 minutes in a saucepan. Add the freshly cooked rice and stir lightly. Remove from the heat, cover, and allow to stand for 10 minutes.

asian-style risotto

Serves **4**
Preparation time **15 minutes**
Cooking time **25 minutes**

5 cups **vegetable stock**
1 tablespoon **dark soy sauce**
2 tablespoons **mirin**
3 tablespoons **sunflower oil**
1 tablespoon **sesame oil**
1 bunch **scallions**, thickly
    sliced
2 **garlic cloves**, chopped
1 inch piece of **fresh ginger
    root**, peeled and grated
2 cups **arborio rice**
6 **Kaffir lime leaves**
8 oz **shiitake mushrooms**
¼ cup chopped **cilantro**, plus
    extra sprigs to garnish

Put the stock, soy sauce, and mirin into a saucepan
and bring to a very gentle simmer.

Meanwhile, heat 2 tablespoons of the sunflower oil
and the sesame oil in a separate saucepan, add the
scallions, garlic, and ginger and cook over a high heat,
stirring, for 1 minute. Add the rice and lime leaves and
cook over a low heat, stirring, for 1 minute until all the
grains are glossy.

Stir about ⅔ cup of the stock into the rice. Cook
over a medium heat, stirring constantly, until absorbed.
Continue to add the stock, a little at a time, and cook,
stirring constantly, until all but a ladleful of stock has
been absorbed.

While the risotto is cooking, wipe the mushrooms,
discard the stalks, and thinly slice all but a few. Heat
the remaining oil in a skillet, add all the mushrooms,
and cook over a medium heat, stirring frequently, for
5 minutes until golden.

Add the cilantro to the risotto with the sliced
mushrooms and the remaining stock. Cook, stirring,
until the stock has been absorbed and the rice is al
dente. Serve garnished with the reserved whole
mushrooms and cilantro sprigs.

For Italian-style risotto, omit the soy sauce, mirin,
sesame oil, and ginger, and use flat mushrooms instead
of shiitake. Stir in 6 tablespoons mascarpone and
4 tablespoons grated Parmesan at the end of cooking
and allow to stand for 5 minutes before serving.

stir-fried tofu with basil & chili

Serves **4**
Preparation time **20 minutes**
Cooking time **6 minutes**

2 tablespoons **sunflower oil**
2 cups cubed **firm tofu**
2 inch piece of **fresh ginger root**, shredded
2 **garlic cloves**, chopped
8 oz **broccoli**, trimmed
8 oz **sugar snap peas**, trimmed
⅔ cup **vegetable stock**
2 tablespoons **sweet chili sauce**
1 tablespoon **light soy sauce**
1 tablespoon **dark soy sauce**
1 tablespoon **lime juice**
2 teaspoons **light brown sugar**
handful of **Thai basil leaves**

Heat half the oil in a wok or deep skillet until smoking, add the tofu, and stir-fry for 2–3 minutes until golden all over. Remove with a slotted spoon.

Add the remaining oil to the pan, add the ginger and garlic and stir-fry for 10 seconds, then add the broccoli and sugar snap peas and stir-fry for 1 minute.

Return the tofu to the pan and add the stock, chili sauce, soy sauces, lime juice, and sugar. Cook for 1 minute until the vegetables are cooked but still crisp. Add the basil leaves and stir well. Serve immediately with rice or noodles.

For tofu & vegetables in oyster sauce, cook the tofu and vegetables as in the recipe above. Return the tofu to the pan and add 3 tablespoons water, cook for 1 minute, then add ⅓ cup oyster sauce and heat through for another minute. Omit the basil and garnish with chopped cilantro.

spinach & ricotta cannelloni

Serves **4**
Preparation time **25 minutes**
Cooking time **35 minutes**

2½ cups frozen **leaf spinach**,
  defrosted
1¼ cups **ricotta cheese**
1 **garlic clove**, crushed
2 tablespoons **light cream**
pinch of freshly grated
  nutmeg
16 **dried cannelloni tubes**
spray oil, for greasing
¼ cup freshly grated
  Parmesan cheese
salt and black pepper

For the tomato salsa
1 lb ripe **tomatoes**, diced
1 **garlic clove**, crushed
½ cup pitted **black olives**,
  chopped
2 tablespoons **capers** in brine,
  drained
1 tablespoon chopped
  parsley
2 tablespoons **extra virgin
  olive oil**

Squeeze the excess water from the spinach and put in a bowl. Add the ricotta, garlic, cream, nutmeg, and salt and pepper, and stir together until evenly combined.

Cook the cannelloni tubes in a large saucepan of boiling water for 5 minutes, or until just al dente. Drain well and immediately refresh under cold water. Pat dry with paper towels.

Lightly grease 4 individual gratin dishes with spray oil. Cut down one side of each cannelloni tube and open out flat. Spoon 2 tablespoons of the spinach and ricotta mixture down one side and roll the pasta up to form tubes once more. Divide between the prepared dishes.

Combine all the salsa ingredients in a bowl, then spoon over the cannelloni. Sprinkle with the Parmesan. Cover the dishes with foil and bake in a preheated oven, 400°F, for 20 minutes. Remove the foil and bake for an additional 10 minutes until bubbling and golden. Serve immediately.

For pumpkin & ricotta cannelloni, steam 1 lb peeled, seeded, and finely diced pumpkin flesh for 10–12 minutes until tender. Allow to cool completely before mixing with the ricotta and other filling ingredients. Continue the recipe as above.

asparagus, tomato, & feta frittata

Serves **4**

Preparation time **10 minutes**,
  plus cooling

Cooking time **about
  40 minutes**

3 tablespoons **olive oil**, plus
  extra for greasing
2 **leeks**, thinly sliced
1 **garlic clove**, crushed
8 oz **asparagus**, trimmed
6 **eggs**
4 oz **feta cheese**, diced
4 tablespoons freshly grated
  Parmesan cheese
6 oz **cherry tomatoes**
salt and black pepper

Heat the oil in a skillet, add the leeks and garlic and cook over a medium heat, stirring frequently, for 10 minutes until tender. Allow to cool.

Cook the asparagus in a large saucepan of lightly salted boiling water for 2 minutes. Drain, refresh under cold water and pat dry. Cut into 2 inch lengths.

Lightly grease an 8 inch square baking dish with olive oil and line the base with nonstick parchment paper. Beat the eggs in a bowl and stir in the leek mixture, asparagus, feta, half the Parmesan, and salt and pepper. Pour the mixture into the prepared dish and top with the tomatoes. Sprinkle with the remaining Parmesan and bake in a preheated oven, 375°F, for 25–30 minutes until puffed up and firm in the center.

Allow to cool in the dish for 10 minutes, then turn out onto a board and serve warm with a crisp green salad.

For mixed mushroom frittata, cook the leeks and garlic as above with 2 teaspoons chopped thyme. Add 4½ cups sliced button mushrooms and cook for an additional 5 minutes. Omit the asparagus and stir the mushrooms into 6 beaten eggs with ½ cup grated Parmesan, 2 tablespoons chopped parsley, and salt and pepper. Bake as above.

potato, chickpea, & cashew curry

Serves **4–6**
Preparation time **20 minutes**
Cooking time **1 hour**

4 tablespoons **vegetable oil**
1 **onion**, sliced
2 **garlic cloves**, crushed
2 teaspoons grated **fresh ginger root**
2 teaspoons ground **coriander**
1 teaspoon ground **cumin**
½ teaspoon ground **turmeric**
½ teaspoon ground **cinnamon**
¼–½ teaspoon **chili powder**
4 ripe **tomatoes**, chopped
1¼ cups **water**
1 lb **potatoes**, cubed
13 oz can **chickpeas**, drained
8 oz **button mushrooms**, trimmed
½ cup **unsalted cashew nuts**
2 tablespoons chopped **cilantro**
⅔ cup **plain yogurt**
salt and black pepper

Heat half the oil in a large saucepan, add the onion, garlic, ginger, spices, and salt and pepper and cook over a low heat, stirring occasionally, for 10 minutes until the onion is softened.

Add the tomatoes and measurement water to the pan and bring to a boil, then reduce the heat, cover, and simmer for 15 minutes. Add the potatoes and chickpeas, cover, and cook for 20 minutes.

Meanwhile, heat the remaining oil in a skillet, add the mushrooms and cook over a medium heat, stirring frequently, for 3–4 minutes until browned.

Add the mushrooms to the curry with the cashew nuts and cilantro and cook for an additional 10 minutes. Stir in the yogurt and heat through without boiling. Serve with rice.

For eggplant & tomato curry, cook the onion, garlic, ginger, and spices as above and stir in a 13 oz can chopped tomatoes. Meanwhile, heat 3 tablespoons vegetable oil in a large skillet, add 1 large diced eggplant and cook over a medium heat, stirring frequently, for 5–6 minutes until golden. Stir into the sauce with the chickpeas and continue as in the recipe above.

onion, pumpkin, & sage pie

Serves **8**

Preparation time **25 minutes**, plus cooling

Cooking time **45–55 minutes**

¼ cup **butter**

1½ lb **onions**, thinly sliced

2 **garlic cloves**, chopped

1 tablespoon chopped **sage**

2 lb **pumpkin**, peeled and seeded

1 tablespoon **olive oil**

2 x 12 oz blocks of **puff pastry**, defrosted if frozen

all-purpose flour, for dusting

8 oz **fontina cheese**, sliced

1 **egg**, beaten

salt and black pepper

Melt the butter in a skillet, add the onions, garlic, sage, and salt and pepper and cook over a medium heat, stirring occasionally, for 20–25 minutes until soft and golden. Allow to cool.

Meanwhile, cut the pumpkin into ¼ inch thick slices and brush with the oil. Heat a ridged griddle pan until hot. Add the pumpkin, in batches, and cook for 2–3 minutes on each side until tender. Allow to cool.

Roll one pastry block out on a lightly floured work surface to form a rectangle a little smaller than a cookie sheet. Lay on the sheet. Spread over half the onion mixture, leaving a 1 inch border. Top with half the pumpkin and half the cheese. Repeat these layers, seasoning with salt and pepper.

Roll out the remaining pastry a little larger than the first. Brush around the filling with beaten egg and top with the second piece of pastry. Press the edges together to seal, then decorate with the tines of a fork. Brush with beaten egg and score the surface with slashes.

Bake in a preheated oven, 425°F, for 25–30 minutes until puffed and golden. Allow to cool slightly, then cut into slices and serve warm.

For pumpkin phyllo pie, layer 4 sheets of phyllo pastry into an 8 x 12 inch baking pan, brushing each with melted butter as you layer. Layer with the ingredients as above, then top with another 4 sheets of phyllo pastry, trimmed to fit the pan, brushing each with butter. Bake for 30 minutes until golden.

soups & stews

curried carrot & lentil soup

Serves **4**
Preparation time **15 minutes**
Cooking time **35 minutes**

2 tablespoons **olive oil**
1 **onion**, chopped
1 **garlic clove**, crushed
1 lb **carrots**, chopped
1 **potato**, chopped
1 tablespoon **medium curry paste**
¾ cup **red split lentils**, washed
4 cups **vegetable stock**
1 tablespoon chopped **cilantro**
salt and black pepper

For the lime oil
4 tablespoons **extra virgin olive oil**
grated zest and juice of **1 lime**

Heat the oil in a saucepan, add the onion and garlic and cook over a medium heat, stirring frequently, for 5 minutes. Add the carrots, potato, and curry paste, stir well and then add the remaining ingredients. Bring to a boil, then reduce the heat, cover, and simmer gently for 25 minutes.

Transfer to a food processor or blender and process until really smooth. Return to the pan and heat through.

Meanwhile, make the lime oil. Beat the ingredients together in a bowl until combined.

Spoon the soup into serving bowls, drizzle over the lime oil, and serve with crusty bread rolls.

For spiced carrot & tomato soup, replace the potato with a 13 oz can chopped tomatoes and add to the soup with the lentils. Stir in ½ teaspoon sugar, then continue as in the recipe above.

mushroom soup with truffle butter

Serves **6**
Preparation time **15 minutes**,
  plus chilling and soaking
Cooking time **40 minutes**

1 tablespoon **dried porcini mushrooms**
4 tablespoons **boiling water**
⅓ cup **butter**
2 **onions**, chopped
2 **garlic cloves**, crushed
2 tablespoons chopped **thyme**
2 lb **flat mushrooms**, trimmed and chopped
4 cups **vegetable stock**
1 cup **light cream**, plus extra to serve
chopped **chives**, to garnish

For the truffle butter
⅔ cup **butter**, softened
2 teaspoons **truffle paste**

First make the truffle butter. Beat the butter and truffle paste together in a bowl until smooth. Form into a log, wrap in plastic wrap, and chill in the freezer for 30 minutes. Cut into slices.

Meanwhile, soak the porcini mushrooms in the measurement water for 15 minutes. Drain well, reserving the soaking liquid, then chop the porcini.

Melt half the butter in a saucepan, add the onions, garlic, and thyme and cook over a low heat, stirring occasionally, for 10 minutes. Add the remaining butter and the fresh mushrooms and porcini and cook over a medium heat, stirring frequently, for 5 minutes, until the mushrooms are softened. Stir in the stock and the reserved soaking liquid and bring to a boil, then reduce the heat, cover, and simmer gently for 20 minutes.

Transfer to a food processor or blender and process until really smooth. Return to the pan, stir in the cream and heat through without boiling. Spoon the soup into serving bowls and serve each portion topped with slices of the truffle butter and chopped chives.

For mushroom, walnut, & thyme soup, replace the cream with milk and omit the truffle butter. Blend the cooked soup, spoon into bowls, and serve drizzled with a little walnut oil. Garnish with a few thyme sprigs and finely chopped walnuts.

chili bean soup

Serves **3–4**
Preparation time **10 minutes**
Cooking time **25 minutes**

2 tablespoons **olive oil**
1 **onion**, chopped
1 **garlic clove**, crushed
1 teaspoon **hot chili powder**
1 teaspoon ground
  coriander
½ teaspoon ground **cumin**
13 oz can **red kidney beans**,
  drained
13 oz can **chopped tomatoes**
2½ cups **vegetable stock**
12 **tortilla chips**
½ cup grated **cheddar cheese**
salt and black pepper
sour cream, to serve

Heat the oil in a saucepan, add the onion, garlic, chili powder, coriander, and cumin and cook over a medium heat, stirring frequently, for 5 minutes until the onion is softened. Add the beans, tomatoes, and stock and season with salt and pepper. Bring to a boil, then reduce the heat, cover, and simmer for 15 minutes.

Transfer to a food processor or blender and process until fairly smooth. Pour into flameproof bowls.

Put the tortilla chips on top of the soup and sprinkle with the cheddar. Cook under a preheated hot broiler for 1–2 minutes until the cheese has melted. Serve immediately with sour cream.

For chili bean soup with low-fat topping, omit the tortilla chip and cheese topping. Split 3 pita breads and cook under a preheated hot broiler until toasted on both sides. Allow to cool slightly, then cut into triangles with kitchen scissors. Serve with the soup, together with a swirl of low-fat plain yogurt instead of the sour cream.

pumpkin soup with olive salsa

Serves **6**
Preparation time **20 minutes**
Cooking time **40 minutes**

4 tablespoons **olive oil**
1 **large onion**, chopped
2 **garlic cloves**, crushed
1 tablespoon chopped **sage**
2 lb peeled, seeded **pumpkin**, cubed
13 oz can **cannellini or haricot beans**, drained
4 cups **vegetable stock**
salt and black pepper

For the olive salsa
½ cup pitted **black olives**
3 tablespoons **extra virgin olive oil**
grated zest of 1 **lemon**
2 tablespoons chopped **parsley**

Heat the oil in a saucepan, add the onion, garlic, and sage and cook over a low heat, stirring frequently, for 5 minutes. Add the pumpkin and beans and stir well, then add the stock and a little salt and pepper.

Bring to a boil, then reduce the heat, cover, and simmer gently for 30 minutes until the pumpkin is tender. Transfer the soup to a food processor or blender and process until smooth. Return to the pan, adjust the seasoning and heat through.

Meanwhile, make the salsa. Chop the olives and mix with the oil, lemon zest, parsley, and salt and pepper in a bowl.

Serve the soup in warmed bowls, topped with spoonfuls of the salsa.

For roasted butternut squash soup, use the same weight of butternut squash instead of pumpkin. Toss the cubes of butternut squash with 1 tablespoon olive oil and roast in a preheated oven, 400°F, for 30 minutes until golden and tender. Continue with the recipe as above, but cook the soup for just 15 minutes.

pea, potato, & arugula soup

Serves **4–6**
Preparation time **15 minutes**
Cooking time **35 minutes**

3 tablespoons **extra virgin
   olive oil**, plus extra to serve
1 **onion**, finely chopped
2 **garlic cloves**, finely
   chopped
2 teaspoons chopped **thyme**
8 oz **potatoes**, chopped
3⅓ cups frozen or fresh
   shelled **peas**
4 cups **vegetable stock**
2½ cups **arugula leaves**,
   roughly chopped
juice of 1 **lemon**
salt and black pepper

Heat the oil in a saucepan, add the onion, garlic, and thyme and cook over a low heat, stirring frequently, for 5 minutes until the onion is softened. Add the potatoes and cook, stirring frequently, for 5 minutes.

Stir in the peas, stock, and salt and pepper. Bring to a boil, then reduce the heat, cover, and simmer gently for 20 minutes.

Transfer the soup to a food processor or blender, add the arugula and lemon juice and process until smooth. Return to the pan, adjust the seasoning, and heat through. Serve immediately, drizzled with a little extra oil.

For summer pea & asparagus soup, omit the potatoes and add 8 oz asparagus spears. Trim off the tips and cook them in the stock for 3–5 minutes, until tender. Drain and set aside, reserving the stock. Slice the remaining asparagus and add to the soup with the peas. Serve garnished with the tips.

winter vegetable & beer broth

Serves **6**
Preparation time **20 minutes**
Cooking time **50–55 minutes**

4 tablespoons **olive oil**
1 **onion**, chopped
2 **garlic cloves**, crushed
1 tablespoon chopped
  rosemary
2 **carrots**, diced
1½ cups diced **parsnips**
1½ cups diced **rutabaga**
½ cup **pearl barley**
2½ cups **beer or lager**
4 cups **vegetable stock**
2 tablespoons chopped
  parsley
salt and black pepper

Heat the oil in a large saucepan, add the onion, garlic, rosemary, carrots, parsnips, and rutabaga and cook over a low heat, stirring frequently, for 10 minutes.

Stir in the barley, beer or lager, stock, and salt and pepper and bring to a boil. Reduce the heat, cover, and simmer gently for 40–45 minutes until the barley and vegetables are tender. Stir in the parsley and adjust the seasoning. Serve with plenty of crusty bread.

For vegetable & rice soup, omit the beer and increase the stock to 6 cups. Replace the barley with an equal quantity of risotto rice. Use 1½ cups diced celeriac instead of the parsnips. Continue the recipe as above. Serve the soup garnished with some more chopped parsley and cracked black pepper.

sweet potato & coconut soup

Serves **4**
Preparation time **15 minutes**
Cooking time **30 minutes**

2 tablespoons **olive oil**
1 **onion**, finely chopped
2 **garlic cloves**, crushed
1 teaspoon grated **fresh ginger root**
grated zest and juice of **1 lime**
1 **red chili**, seeded and chopped
1½ lb **sweet potatoes**, peeled and roughly chopped
2½ cups **vegetable stock**
13 oz can **coconut milk**
3 cups **baby spinach leaves**
salt and black pepper

Heat the oil in a saucepan, add the onion, garlic, ginger, lime zest, and chili and cook over a low heat, stirring frequently, for 5 minutes until the onion is softened. Add the sweet potatoes and cook, stirring frequently, for 5 minutes.

Stir in the stock, coconut milk, lime juice, and salt and pepper. Bring to a boil, then reduce the heat, cover, and simmer gently for 15 minutes, or until the potatoes are tender.

Transfer half the soup to a food processor or blender and process until smooth. Return to the pan, stir in the spinach, and cook until just wilted. Adjust the seasoning and serve immediately.

For creamy pumpkin, cilantro, & coconut soup, replace the sweet potato with an equal quantity of peeled, seeded, and diced pumpkin. Cook the soup for 20 minutes, then process in a food processor or blender until smooth, adding 2 tablespoons chopped cilantro instead of the spinach. Finish the recipe as above.

pasta & bean soup with basil oil

Serves **6**
Preparation time **15 minutes**
Cooking time **35 minutes**

2 tablespoons **extra virgin
 olive oil**
1 **onion**, chopped
3 **garlic cloves**, crushed
1 tablespoon chopped
 rosemary
2 x 13 oz cans **chopped
 tomatoes**
2½ cups **vegetable stock**
13 oz can **borlotti beans**,
 drained
4 oz **dried small pasta
 shapes**
salt and black pepper
grated **Parmesan cheese**,
 to serve

For the basil oil
½ cup **basil leaves**
⅔ cup **extra virgin olive oil**

Heat the oil in saucepan, add the onion, garlic, and rosemary and cook over a low heat, stirring frequently, for 5 minutes until the onion is softened.

Stir in the tomatoes, stock, beans, and salt and pepper. Bring to a boil, then reduce the heat, cover, and simmer gently for 20 minutes. Add the pasta and simmer, covered, for an additional 10 minutes until the pasta is al dente.

Meanwhile, make the basil oil. Plunge the basil leaves into a saucepan of boiling water, return to a boil, and boil for 30 seconds. Drain the basil, refresh under cold water and dry thoroughly with paper towels. Transfer the oil and basil leaves to a blender and blend until really smooth.

Ladle the soup into bowls and spoon a little of the basil oil over each serving. Serve immediately, sprinkled with some grated Parmesan.

For spiced tomato & Mexican bean soup, replace the rosemary with thyme and the borlotti beans with a drained 13 oz can of red kidney beans. Continue as above, omitting the pasta and adding 2 tablespoons chili sauce to the soup. Serve the soup topped with sour cream.

mushroom ramen

Serves **4**
Preparation time **10 minutes**
Cooking time **15 minutes**

10 oz **dried ramen noodles**
6 cups **vegetable stock**
5 tablespoons **dark soy sauce**
3 tablespoons **mirin**
12 oz **mixed mushrooms**, trimmed
4 **scallions**, trimmed and thinly sliced
1¼ cups **silken tofu**, drained and diced

Cook the noodles according to the package instructions. Drain well in a colander, refresh under cold water and set aside.

Combine the stock, soy sauce, and mirin in a saucepan and bring to a boil, then reduce the heat and simmer gently for 5 minutes. Add the mushrooms and simmer gently for an additional 5 minutes. Add the scallions and tofu.

Meanwhile, boil a full kettle of water. Set the noodles, still in the colander, over a sink and pour over the boiling water. Divide the noodles between serving bowls and add the soup. Serve immediately.

For vegetable ramen, omit the mushrooms and replace with 4 oz broccoli florets, 4 oz sugar snap peas and 4 oz trimmed asparagus, cut into short lengths. Simmer in the broth for 3 minutes and continue as in the recipe above. Ramen noodles are available from Japanese food stores and most health-food stores.

saffron-scented vegetable tagine

Serves **4**
Preparation time **15 minutes**
Cooking time **50 minutes**

½ cup **sunflower oil**
1 large **onion**, finely chopped
2 **garlic cloves**, crushed
2 teaspoons ground
  coriander
2 teaspoons ground **cumin**
2 teaspoons ground
  cinnamon
13 oz can **chickpeas**, drained
13 oz can **chopped tomatoes**
2½ cups **vegetable stock**
¼ teaspoon **saffron threads**
1 large **eggplant**, trimmed and
  chopped
8 oz **button mushrooms**,
  trimmed and halved if large
5 **dried figs**, chopped
2 tablespoons chopped
  cilantro
salt and black pepper

Heat 2 tablespoons of the oil in a skillet, add the onion, garlic, and spices and cook over a medium heat, stirring frequently, for 5 minutes until golden. Using a slotted spoon, transfer to a saucepan and add the chickpeas, tomatoes, stock, and saffron. Season with salt and pepper.

Heat the remaining oil in the skillet, add the eggplant and cook over a high heat, stirring frequently, for 5 minutes until browned. Add to the stew and bring to a boil, then reduce the heat, cover, and simmer gently for 20 minutes.

Stir in the mushrooms and figs and simmer gently, uncovered, for an additional 20 minutes. Stir in the cilantro and adjust the seasoning. Serve with steamed couscous.

For winter vegetable & lentil tagine, replace the eggplant with 2 sliced carrots and 2 cubed potatoes. Instead of the chickpeas use a drained 13 oz can of green lentils. Follow the recipe above and stir in ½ cup dried apricots instead of the figs.

goulash with chive dumplings

Serves **4**

Preparation time **30 minutes**

Cooking time **45 minutes**

4 tablespoons **olive oil**

8 **baby onions**, peeled

2 **garlic cloves**, crushed

1 **carrot**, chopped

1 large **celery stick**, sliced

1 lb **potatoes**, cubed

1 teaspoon **caraway seeds**

1 teaspoon **smoked paprika**

13 oz can **chopped tomatoes**

2 cups **vegetable stock**

salt and black pepper

For the chive dumplings

¾ cup **self-rising flour**

½ teaspoon **salt**

½ cup **vegetarian suet**

1 tablespoon chopped **chives**

4–5 tablespoons **water**

Heat the oil in a large saucepan, add the onions, garlic, carrot, celery, potatoes, and caraway seeds and cook over a medium heat, stirring frequently, for 10 minutes. Add the paprika and cook, stirring, for 1 minute.

Stir in the tomatoes, stock, and salt and pepper. Bring to a boil, then reduce the heat, cover, and simmer gently for 20 minutes.

Make the dumplings. Sift the flour and salt into a bowl and stir in the suet, chives, and pepper to taste. Working quickly and lightly, gradually mix in enough of the measurement water to form a soft dough. Divide into 8 equal pieces and roll into balls.

Carefully arrange the dumplings in the stew, leaving gaps between them, cover, and simmer for 15 minutes until doubled in size and light and fluffy.

For horseradish dumplings, follow the method above, using 2 teaspoons grated fresh horseradish instead of the chopped chives. Continue with the recipe as above. These dumplings are especially good with beets: omit the tomatoes, increase the stock to 2½ cups and add 9 oz cooked beets.

provençal vegetable stew

Serves **4**
Preparation time **15 minutes**
Cooking time **55 minutes**

4 tablespoons **extra virgin olive oil**, plus extra for drizzling
1 large **red onion**, sliced
4 **garlic cloves**, chopped
2 teaspoons **ground coriander**
1 tablespoon chopped **thyme**
1 **fennel bulb**, trimmed and sliced
1 **red bell pepper**, cored, seeded, and sliced
1 lb **vine-ripened tomatoes**, diced
1¼ cups **vegetable stock**
⅔ cup **Niçoise olives**
2 tablespoons chopped **parsley**
slices of **crusty bread**
salt and black pepper

Heat the oil in a large saucepan, add the onion, garlic, coriander, and thyme and cook over a medium heat, stirring frequently, for 5 minutes until the onion is softened. Add the fennel and bell pepper and cook, stirring frequently, for 10 minutes until softened.

Stir in the tomatoes, stock, and salt and pepper. Bring to a boil, then reduce the heat, cover, and simmer gently for 30 minutes. Stir in the olives and parsley and simmer, uncovered, for an additional 10 minutes.

Meanwhile, heat a ridged griddle pan until hot. Add the bread slices and cook until toasted and charred on both sides. Drizzle liberally with oil.

Serve the stew hot with the toasted bread.

For pasta with Provençal sauce, cook 1 lb dried penne in a large saucepan of lightly salted boiling water for 10–12 minutes, or according to the package instructions, until al dente. Drain well and top the pasta with the vegetable stew, used as a pasta sauce.

fennel, pernod, & orange casserole

Serves **4**
Preparation time **15 minutes**
Cooking time **about 50 minutes**

2 **fennel bulbs**, trimmed
4 tablespoons **extra virgin olive oil**
1 **onion**, chopped
2 **garlic cloves**, crushed
2 teaspoons chopped **rosemary**
salt and black pepper
6 tablespoons **Pernod**
13 oz can **chopped tomatoes**
¼ teaspoon **saffron threads**
2 strips of **orange peel**
2 tablespoons chopped **fennel fronds**
Chargrilled Polenta Triangles, to serve (see page 170)

Cut the fennel lengthwise into ¼ inch thick slices. Heat half the oil in a flameproof casserole, add the fennel slices, in batches, and cook over a medium heat for 3–4 minutes on each side until golden. Remove with a slotted spoon.

Heat the remaining oil in the casserole, add the onion, garlic, rosemary, and salt and pepper and cook over a low heat, stirring frequently, for 5 minutes. Add the Pernod, bring to a boil, and boil until reduced by half. Add the tomatoes, saffron, and orange peel, and stir well. Arrange the fennel slices over the top.

Bring the casserole to a boil, then cover with a tight-fitting lid and bake in a preheated oven, 350°F, for 35 minutes until the fennel is tender. Stir in the fennel fronds and serve the casserole hot with some Chargrilled Polenta Triangles.

For fennel gratin, prepare the fennel casserole as in the recipe above and transfer to a gratin dish. Combine 2 cups fresh white bread crumbs, 4 tablespoons grated Parmesan, and 2 tablespoons chopped parsley. Sprinkle over the top of the fennel mixture and bake, uncovered, for 35 minutes.

home baked beans

Serves **4–6**
Preparation time **10 minutes**
Cooking time **about 2 hours**

2 x 13 oz cans **borlotti beans**,
  drained
1 **garlic clove**, crushed
1 **onion**, finely chopped
2 cups **vegetable stock**
1¼ cups **passata** (sieved
  tomatoes)
2 tablespoons **molasses**
2 tablespoons **tomato paste**
2 tablespoons **dark brown
  sugar**
1 tablespoon **Dijon mustard**
1 tablespoon **red wine
  vinegar**
salt and black pepper

Put all the ingredients in a flameproof casserole with a little salt and pepper. Cover and bring slowly to a boil.

Bake in a preheated oven, 325°F, for 1½ hours. Remove the lid and bake for an additional 30 minutes until the sauce is syrupy. Serve with hot buttered toast.

For home baked beans with baked potatoes, scrub 4 baking potatoes, about 8 oz each, then bake in a preheated oven, 400°F, for about 1 hour until cooked through. Cut lengthwise in half, season with salt and pepper, and spoon the beans over. Grate over a little cheddar before serving. The home baked beans are even better made a day ahead and heated through before serving.

salads & sides

tomato, avocado, & peach salad

Serves **4**
Preparation time **15 minutes**,
  plus cooling
Cooking time **20 minutes**

4 **plum tomatoes**, sliced
1 **avocado**, peeled, pitted,
  and sliced
8 oz **buffalo mozzarella
  cheese**, sliced
1 ripe **peach**, pitted and diced
⅓ cup pitted **black olives**
1 **red chili**, seeded and finely
  chopped
3 tablespoons **extra virgin
  olive oil**, plus extra for
  drizzling
juice of 1 **lime**
1 tablespoon chopped
  cilantro
salt and black pepper

For the balsamic glaze
2½ cups **balsamic vinegar**

First make the balsamic glaze. Pour the vinegar into a saucepan and bring to a boil. Reduce the heat and simmer gently for 20 minutes, or until reduced to about ⅔ cup. Allow to cool completely.

Arrange the tomatoes, avocado, and mozzarella on a large platter. Combine the peach, olives, chili, oil, lime juice, cilantro, and salt and pepper in a bowl, stir well, and spoon over the salad.

Drizzle the salad with a little extra oil and the balsamic glaze and serve.

For classic Italian tricolore salad, arrange 4 sliced tomatoes, 1 sliced avocado, 8 oz sliced buffalo mozzarella, and a few torn basil leaves on a platter. Drizzle over some extra virgin olive oil and a little white wine vinegar, and season with salt and cracked black pepper.

charred leek salad with hazelnuts

Serves **4**
Preparation time **10 minutes**
Cooking time **12–16 minutes**

1 lb **baby leeks**
1–2 tablespoons
   hazelnut oil
dash of **lemon juice**
⅛ cup blanched **hazelnuts**
2 Little Gem or romaine
   lettuce hearts
a few **mint sprigs**
½ oz **pecorino cheese**
20 **black olives**, to garnish

For the dressing
4 tablespoons **hazelnut oil**
2 tablespoons **extra virgin**
   olive oil
2 teaspoons **sherry vinegar**
salt and black pepper

Brush the leeks with the hazelnut oil. Cook, in batches, on a preheated hot ridged griddle pan or under a preheated hot broiler, turning frequently, for 6–8 minutes until evenly browned and cooked through. Toss with the lemon juice and season with salt and pepper. Allow to cool.

Meanwhile, heat a heavy skillet until hot, add the hazelnuts, and cook over a medium heat, stirring, for 3–4 minutes until browned. Allow to cool slightly and then roughly chop. Separate the lettuce leaves and pull the mint leaves from the sprigs.

Arrange the leeks in serving bowls or on plates and top with the lettuce leaves, mint, and hazelnuts. Beat all the dressing ingredients together in a small bowl, season with salt and pepper, and pour over the salad. Shave the pecorino over the salad and serve garnished with the olives.

For charred asparagus salad with pine nuts, replace the leeks with the same quantity of trimmed asparagus. Brush with extra virgin olive oil rather than hazelnut oil, and cook and dress as in the recipe above. Toast pine nuts instead of hazelnuts, and use tarragon leaves in place of mint. For the dressing, use 4 tablespoons extra virgin olive oil, 2 tablespoons grapeseed oil, 2 teaspoons tarragon vinegar, and the grated zest of 1 lemon, reserving a few thin strips of peel. Shave a little Parmesan over the salad and garnish with the reserved lemon peel strips.

watermelon, fennel, & feta salad

Serves **4**
Preparation time **10 minutes**
Cooking time **2 minutes**

2 cups fresh or frozen shelled
   fava beans
1 large **fennel bulb**
1⅔ cups diced **watermelon
   flesh**
4 oz **feta cheese**, crumbled
salt and black pepper

For the dressing
3 tablespoons **extra virgin
   olive oil**
1 tablespoon **lemon juice**
1 teaspoon **honey**
1 teaspoon **pomegranate
   syrup**

Cook the beans in a large saucepan of lightly salted boiling water for 2 minutes. Drain and immediately refresh under cold water. Pat dry with paper towels, then peel off and discard the tough outer skins. Put the beans in a bowl.

Trim the fennel bulb. Cut in half, then crosswise into wafer-thin slices. Add to the beans with the watermelon and feta.

Beat all the dressing ingredients together in a small bowl and season with salt and pepper. Pour over the salad, toss well, and serve.

For fennel, orange, & parsley salad, very thinly slice a large fennel bulb into a bowl and add ½ bunch of parsley, 2 tablespoons drained baby capers, and 1 peeled and segmented orange. Add the juice of ½ lemon, 1 tablespoon orange juice, and a good spoonful of extra virgin olive oil. Season with salt and pepper and mix well to combine.

spiced couscous salad

Serves **4**

Preparation time **15 minutes**, plus soaking

Cooking time **3 minutes**

¾ cup **vegetable stock**

¾ cup **orange juice**

1 teaspoon ground **cinnamon**

½ teaspoon ground **coriander**

1½ cups **couscous**

½ cup **raisins**

2 ripe **tomatoes**, chopped

¼ **preserved lemon**, chopped (optional)

½ bunch **parsley**, roughly chopped

½ bunch **mint**, roughly chopped

1 **garlic clove**, crushed

4 tablespoons **extra virgin olive oil**

salt and black pepper

Combine the stock, orange juice, spices, and ½ teaspoon salt in a saucepan. Bring to a boil and stir in the couscous. Remove from the heat, cover, and allow to soak for 10 minutes.

Put the raisins, tomatoes, preserved lemon, if using, herbs, garlic, and oil in a large bowl and toss well. Stir in the soaked couscous and season with salt and pepper. Serve warm or allow to cool and serve at room temperature.

For couscous tabbouleh, follow the recipe above for the first step, then stir in 4 chopped ripe tomatoes, ½ diced cucumber, 1 small diced red onion, ½ bunch each of chopped parsley and mint, 4 tablespoons extra virgin olive oil, the juice of 1 lemon, and salt and pepper to taste. Toss well and taste, adding more lemon juice, if you desire.

middle eastern bread salad

Serves **4–6**

Preparation time **10 minutes**,
plus cooling

2 **flatbreads or flour tortillas**
1 large **green bell pepper**,
cored, seeded, and diced
1 **Lebanese cucumber**, diced
8 oz **cherry tomatoes**, halved
½ **red onion**, finely chopped
2 tablespoons chopped **mint**
2 tablespoons chopped
parsley
2 tablespoons chopped
cilantro
3 tablespoons **extra virgin
olive oil**
juice of 1 **lemon**
salt and black pepper

Cook the flatbreads on a preheated ridged griddle pan or under a preheated hot broiler for 2–3 minutes until toasted and charred. Allow to cool, then tear into bite-size pieces.

Put the bell pepper, cucumber, tomatoes, onion, and herbs in a bowl, add the oil, lemon juice, and salt and pepper and stir well. Add the bread and stir again. Serve immediately.

For tomato & bread salad, chop 1½ lb ripe tomatoes into a bowl and add 4 slices of diced day-old bread, 1 bunch of basil leaves, ⅔ cup pitted black olives, 5 tablespoons extra virgin olive oil, 1 tablespoon balsamic vinegar, and salt and pepper. Toss well and serve.

new potato, basil, & pine nut salad

Serves **4–6**
Preparation time **5 minutes**,
   plus cooling
Cooking time **15 minutes**

2 lb **new potatoes**, scrubbed
4 tablespoons **extra virgin
   olive oil**
1½ tablespoons **white wine
   vinegar**
⅛ cup **pine nuts**, toasted
½ bunch **basil leaves**
salt and black pepper

Put the potatoes in a large saucepan of lightly salted water and bring to a boil. Cook for 12–15 minutes until tender. Drain well and transfer to a large bowl. Cut any large potatoes in half.

Beat the oil, vinegar, and a little salt and pepper together in a small bowl. Add half to the potatoes, stir well, and allow to cool completely.

Add the pine nuts, the remaining dressing, and basil, stir well and serve.

For traditional potato salad, cook 2 lb new potatoes as above, drain, and allow to cool. Combine ⅔ cup good-quality mayonnaise with 1 bunch of finely chopped scallions, 2 tablespoons chopped fresh chives, a squeeze of lemon juice, and salt and pepper. Toss with the potatoes.

spinach & gorgonzola salad

Serves **4**

Preparation time **5 minutes**, plus cooling

Cooking time **3 minutes**

1 tablespoon **honey**

1 cup **walnut halves**

8 oz **green beans**, trimmed

4 cups **baby spinach leaves**

5 oz **Gorgonzola cheese**, crumbled

For the dressing

4 tablespoons **walnut oil**

2 tablespoons **extra virgin olive oil**

1–2 tablespoons **sherry vinegar**

salt and black pepper

Heat the honey in a small skillet, add the walnuts, and stir-fry over a medium heat for 2–3 minutes until the nuts are glazed. Tip onto a plate and allow to cool.

Meanwhile, cook the beans in a saucepan of lightly salted boiling water for 3 minutes. Drain, refresh under cold water and shake dry. Put in a large bowl with the spinach leaves.

Beat all the dressing ingredients together in a small bowl and season with salt and pepper. Pour over the salad and toss well. Arrange the salad in serving bowls, sprinkle with the Gorgonzola and glazed walnuts, and serve immediately.

For watercress, almond, & Stilton salad, replace the spinach with an equal amount of watercress. Dress with ½ cup toasted slivered almonds, 7 oz crumbled Stilton instead of the Gorgonzola, and a drizzle of olive oil.

greek country salad with haloumi

Serves **4**
Preparation time **10 minutes**
Cooking time **2 minutes**

4 **vine-ripened tomatoes**,
  roughly chopped
½ **onion**, sliced
1 **Lebanese cucumber**,
  thickly sliced
½ cup pitted **black Kalamata
  olives**
1 small **romaine lettuce**
8 oz **haloumi cheese**, sliced

For the dressing
4 tablespoons **extra virgin
  olive oil**
1½ tablespoons **red wine
  vinegar**
1 teaspoon **dried oregano**
salt and black pepper

Put the tomatoes, onion, cucumber, and olives in a bowl. Tear the lettuce into pieces and add to the salad. Toss well and arrange on a large platter.

Beat all the dressing ingredients together in a small bowl and season with salt and pepper. Drizzle a little over the salad.

Heat a heavy skillet until hot, add the haloumi slices and cook for 1 minute on each side until charred and softened. Arrange on top of the salad, drizzle over the remaining dressing and serve immediately.

For Greek salad with chunky croutons, replace the haloumi with 7 oz crumbled feta cheese. To make the croutons, cut thick slices of close-textured country bread, then cut these into large chunks. Heat a little olive oil in a skillet and fry the bread, turning occasionally, until crisp and golden. Add extra olive oil as needed. Cool, then toss into the salad and serve immediately.

fig, bean, & toasted pecan salad

Serves **4**

Preparation time **5 minutes**, plus cooling

Cooking time **5–6 minutes**

1 cup **pecan nuts**

7 oz **green beans**, trimmed

4 ripe fresh **figs**, cut into quarters

2 cups **arugula leaves**

small handful of **mint leaves**

2 oz **Parmesan or pecorino cheese**

For the dressing

3 tablespoons **walnut oil**

2 teaspoons **sherry vinegar**

1 teaspoon **vincotto**

salt and black pepper

Heat a heavy skillet until hot, add the pecan nuts and cook over a medium heat, stirring, for 3–4 minutes until browned. Allow to cool.

Cook the beans in a saucepan of lightly salted boiling water for 2 minutes. Drain, refresh under cold water and pat dry with paper towels. Put the beans in a bowl with the figs, pecan nuts, arugula, and mint.

Beat all the dressing ingredients together in a small bowl and season with salt and pepper. Pour over the salad and toss well. Shave over the Parmesan or pecorino.

For mixed bean salad, combine 7 oz cooked trimmed green beans with 2 x 13 oz cans drained mixed beans, 4 finely chopped scallions, 1 crushed garlic clove, and 4 tablespoons chopped mixed herbs, then dress with 4 tablespoons extra virgin olive oil, juice of ½ lemon, a pinch of superfine sugar, and salt and pepper. If you can't find vincotto (see page 13), use balsamic vinegar as an alternative.

thai vegetable salad

Serves **4**

Preparation time **10 minutes**, plus cooling

Cooking time **2 minutes**

8 oz **cherry tomatoes**, quartered

1 **Lebanese cucumber**, thinly sliced

1 **green papaya or green mango**

1 large **red chili**, seeded and thinly sliced

2½ cups **bean sprouts**

4 **scallions**, trimmed and thinly sliced

small handful of **Thai basil leaves**

small handful of **mint leaves**

small handful of **cilantro leaves**

4 tablespoons **unsalted peanuts**, roughly chopped

For the chili dressing

2 tablespoons **Chili Jam** (see page 44)

2 tablespoons **light soy sauce**

2 tablespoons **lime juice**

4 teaspoons grated **palm sugar**

First make the dressing. Put all the ingredients in a small saucepan and warm over a low heat, stirring, until the sugar has dissolved. Allow to cool.

Put the tomatoes, cucumber, papaya or mango, chili, bean sprouts, scallions, and herbs in a bowl. Add the dressing and toss well. Transfer to a platter. Sprinkle with the peanuts and serve immediately.

For Thai salad wraps, serve the salad with large iceberg lettuce leaves. Spoon a little salad onto the leaves, roll up and dip into the chili dressing. To cool the chili heat, make a dressing of soy sauce, lime juice, and omit the palm sugar. Omit the chili jam but add 2 tablespoons warmed lime marmalade instead.

roast vegetables & parsley pesto

Serves **4**

Preparation time **15 minutes**

Cooking time **50 minutes–1 hour**

4 small **potatoes**, scrubbed

1 **red onion**

2 **carrots**

2 **parsnips**

8 **garlic cloves**, unpeeled

4 **thyme sprigs**

2 tablespoons **extra virgin olive oil**

For the parsley pesto

½ cup blanched **almonds**

large bunch **flat leaf parsley**

2 **garlic cloves**, chopped

⅔ cup **extra virgin olive oil**

2 tablespoons grated **Parmesan cheese**

salt and black pepper

Cut the potatoes and onion into wedges and the carrots and parsnips into quarters. Put in a large roasting pan to fit in a single layer. Add the garlic cloves, thyme sprigs, oil, and salt and pepper and stir well until evenly coated. Roast in a preheated oven, 425°F, for 50 minutes–1 hour until browned and tender, stirring halfway through.

Meanwhile, make the pesto. Heat a heavy skillet until hot, add the almonds, and cook over a medium heat, stirring, for 3–4 minutes until browned. Transfer to a bowl and allow to cool.

Put the almonds in a mortar or food processor, add the parsley, garlic, and salt and pepper and grind with a pestle or process to form a coarse paste. Transfer to a bowl, stir in the oil and Parmesan and adjust the seasoning.

Serve the roast vegetables hot with the pesto.

For pasta with parsley pesto, cook 1 lb dried pasta in a large saucepan of lightly salted boiling water according to the package instructions, until al dente. Meanwhile, make the pesto. Drain the pasta, reserving 4 tablespoons of the cooking water. Return the pasta and the reserved pasta cooking water to the pan. Add the pesto, toss well and serve. The pasta can be served as a substantial base for the roast vegetables.

spiced braised new potatoes

Serves **4–6**
Preparation time **15 minutes**
Cooking time **45 minutes**

¼ cup **butter**
1 small **onion**, finely chopped
1 **garlic clove**, crushed
1 teaspoon grated **fresh ginger root**
1 teaspoon ground **coriander**
½ teaspoon ground **turmeric**
½ teaspoon ground **cumin**
2 lb small **waxy potatoes**, scrubbed
1¼ cups **vegetable stock**
2 ripe **tomatoes**, diced
chopped **cilantro**, to garnish
salt and black pepper

Melt the butter in a saucepan, add the onion, garlic, ginger, and spices and cook over a low heat, stirring frequently, for 5 minutes. Add the potatoes and salt and pepper, stir well, and then add the stock and tomatoes to the pan.

Bring to a boil, then reduce the heat, cover, and simmer gently for 20 minutes.

Remove the lid and simmer, uncovered, for an additional 15–20 minutes until the liquid is reduced and thickened to a glaze. Serve hot, garnished with some chopped fresh cilantro.

For roasted new potatoes with garlic & rosemary,
put 2 lb scrubbed small waxy potatoes into a roasting pan with 12 whole unpeeled garlic cloves, 2 tablespoons chopped rosemary, 2 tablespoons olive oil, and salt and pepper. Stir well and roast in a preheated oven, 400°F, for 40–45 minutes until tender.

vegetable tempura

Serves **4**
Preparation time **20 minutes**
Cooking time **about
  20 minutes**

2 cups **broccoli florets**
1 cup **red bell pepper slices**
1 cup **pumpkin slices**
1 cup **trimmed green beans**
¼ cup **zucchini slices**
vegetable oil, for deep-frying

For the dipping sauce
1 cup **vegetable stock**
1 tablespoon **wakame
  seaweed** (see page 13)
3 tablespoons **mirin**
3 tablespoons **dark soy
  sauce**

For the tempura batter
1 **egg yolk**
1 cup **cold water**
1¼ cups **all-purpose flour**

First make the dipping sauce. Put all the ingredients in a saucepan and heat over a low heat without boiling for 10 minutes. Keep warm.

Meanwhile, heat 2 inches vegetable oil in a wok or deep, heavy saucepan until it reaches 350–375°F, or until a cube of bread browns in 30 seconds.

Quickly beat all the batter ingredients together in a bowl. Dip the vegetables in the batter, a few at a time, add to the hot oil and deep-fry for 2–3 minutes until crisp and lightly browned. Remove with a slotted spoon and drain on paper towels. Keep warm in a moderate oven while cooking the remainder.

Serve the vegetable tempura with the dipping sauce.

For ponzu dipping sauce, combine 2 tablespoons dark soy sauce, 4 tablespoons rice wine vinegar, and 1 tablespoon lemon juice, and serve with the vegetable tempura.

baked sweet potatoes

Serves **4**
Preparation time **5 minutes**
Cooking time **45–50 minutes**

4 **sweet potatoes**, about
  8 oz each, scrubbed
¾ cup **sour cream**
2 **scallions**, trimmed and
  finely chopped
1 tablespoon chopped **chives**
¼ cup **butter**
salt and black pepper

Put the potatoes in a roasting pan and roast in a preheated oven, 425°F, for 45–50 minutes until cooked through.

Meanwhile, combine the sour cream, scallions, chives, and salt and pepper in a bowl.

Cut the baked potatoes in half lengthwise, top with the butter and spoon over the sour cream mixture. Serve immediately.

For crispy sweet potato skins, allow the baked sweet potatoes to cool, cut into wedges, and cut out some of the soft potato, leaving a good lining inside the skin. Deep-fry in hot oil for 4–5 minutes until crisp. Serve with sour cream and chopped chives to dip.

indian-spiced pumpkin wedges

Serves **4**
Preparation time **15 minutes**, plus cooling
Cooking time **15–20 minutes**

2 lb **pumpkin or butternut squash**
1 teaspoon **cumin seeds**
1 teaspoon **coriander seeds**
2 **cardamom pods**
3 tablespoons **sunflower oil**
1 teaspoon **superfine sugar or mango chutney**

For the coconut pesto
½ cup **cilantro leaves**
1 **garlic clove**, crushed
1 **green chili**, seeded and chopped
pinch of **superfine sugar**
1 tablespoon **pistachio nuts**, roughly chopped
6 tablespoons **coconut cream**
1 tablespoon **lime juice**
salt and black pepper

Cut the pumpkin or squash into thin wedges about ½ inch thick, discarding the seeds and fibers, and put in a large dish.

Heat a heavy skillet until hot, add the whole spices and cook over a medium heat, stirring, until browned. Allow to cool, then grind to a powder in a spice grinder or in a mortar with a pestle. Mix the ground spices with the oil and sugar or mango chutney in a small bowl, then add to the pumpkin wedges and toss well to coat.

Cook the pumpkin or squash wedges under a preheated hot broiler, or over a preheated hot gas barbecue or the hot coals of a charcoal barbecue, for 6–8 minutes on each side until charred and tender.

Meanwhile, make the pesto. Put the cilantro leaves, garlic, chili, sugar, and pistachio nuts in a food processor and process until fairly finely ground and blended. Season with salt and pepper. Add the coconut cream and lime juice and process again. Transfer to a serving bowl.

Serve the wedges hot with the coconut pesto.

For Indian-spiced sweet potato wedges, cook 4 scrubbed sweet potatoes, 8 oz each, in a large saucepan of simmering water for 15 minutes, or until just tender, then drain. When cool enough to handle, slice into large wedges. Toss with the spice and oil mixture and broil or barbecue, as above, for about 6 minutes, turning frequently, until browned. Serve hot with the coconut pesto.

chargrilled polenta triangles

Serves **8**

Preparation time **5 minutes**, plus cooling

Cooking time **15–20 minutes**

spray oil, for greasing

4 cups **water**

2 teaspoons **salt**

1 cup **instant polenta**

2 **garlic cloves**, crushed

¼ cup **butter**

½ cup freshly grated **Parmesan cheese**, plus extra to serve

olive oil, for brushing

chopped **fresh parsley**, to garnish

black pepper

Lightly grease a 9 x 12 inch baking pan with spray oil. Bring the measurement water to a boil in a heavy saucepan, add the salt and then gradually beat in the polenta in a steady stream. Cook over a low heat, stirring constantly with a wooden spoon, for 5 minutes until the grains have swelled and thickened.

Remove from the heat and immediately beat in the garlic, butter, Parmesan, and pepper until smooth. Pour the mixture into the prepared pan and allow to cool.

Turn the polenta out onto a cutting board and cut into large squares, then diagonally in half into triangles. Brush the triangles with a little oil.

Heat a ridged griddle pan until hot. Add the polenta triangles, in batches, and cook over a medium-high heat for 2–3 minutes on each side until charred and heated through. Serve immediately, garnished with grated Parmesan and chopped parsley.

For soft polenta with sage butter, melt ½ cup butter in a small saucepan. Add 1 tablespoon chopped sage and a pinch of cayenne pepper to the butter and cook over a medium-high heat, stirring, for 2–3 minutes until the sage is crisp and the butter turns golden brown. Keep warm. Follow the above recipe to the end of the first stage. Remove the cooked polenta from the heat and stir in ½ cup grated Parmesan. Pour into bowls and serve drizzled with the sage butter.

breads & baking

fig, goat cheese, & tapenade tart

Serves **4**

Preparation time **10 minutes**

Cooking time **20–25 minutes**

12 oz **puff pastry**, defrosted
    if frozen

all-purpose flour, for dusting

1 **egg**, beaten

3 tablespoons ready-made
    olive tapenade

3 fresh ripe **figs**, quartered

8 **cherry tomatoes**, halved

4 oz **soft goat cheese**,
    crumbled

2 teaspoons chopped **thyme**

2 tablespoons freshly grated
    Parmesan cheese

Arugula Salad, to serve (see
    page 56) (optional)

Roll the pastry out on a lightly floured work surface until ¼ inch thick to form a rectangle 8 x 12 inches, trimming the edges. Prick the pastry with a fork and score a border 1 inch in from the edges. Transfer to a baking sheet. Brush the pastry with a little beaten egg and bake in a preheated oven, 400°F, for 12–15 minutes.

Remove the pastry from the oven and carefully press down the center to flatten slightly. Spread the center with the tapenade and then arrange the figs, tomatoes, goat cheese, thyme, and Parmesan over the top.

Return the tart to the oven and bake for an additional 5–10 minutes until the pastry is golden, the cheese is melted and the figs are cooked. Brown the top under a preheated hot broiler, if desired, making sure that the pastry edges don't burn (you can cover them with foil). Serve warm with an arugula salad, if wished.

For broiled vegetable & goat cheese tart, thinly slice 1 zucchini and 1 eggplant, core, seed, and quarter 1 red bell pepper and cut 1 red onion into thin wedges. Brush the vegetables with olive oil and cook under a preheated hot broiler for 3–4 minutes on each side until tender. Use the broiled vegetables in place of the figs and tomatoes, and continue with the recipe as above.

mixed mushroom tart

Serves **6**
Preparation time **45 minutes**,
  plus chilling and cooling
Cooking time **50–55 minutes**

¼ cup **butter**
6 **shallots**, finely chopped
2 **garlic cloves**, crushed
2 teaspoons chopped **thyme**
12 oz mixed **mushrooms**,
  such as shiitake, oyster,
  brown, and field, trimmed
  and sliced
1¼ cups **sour cream**
3 **eggs**, lightly beaten
¼ cup freshly grated
  Parmesan cheese
salt and black pepper
arugula leaves, to serve

For the pastry
1¾ cups **all-purpose flour**,
  plus extra for dusting
½ teaspoon **salt**
½ cup chilled **unsalted butter**,
  diced
1 **egg yolk**
2 tablespoons **cold water**

First make the pastry. Sift the flour and salt into a bowl. Add the butter and blend with the fingertips until the mixture resembles fine bread crumbs. Add the egg yolk and measurement water and bring the mixture together. Wrap in plastic wrap and chill for 30 minutes.

Roll the pastry out on a lightly floured work surface. Use to line a 10 inch fluted tart pan. Prick the base with a fork and chill for 30 minutes. Line the pastry with nonstick parchment paper and pie weights and bake in a preheated oven, 400°F, for 15 minutes. Remove the paper and weights and bake for an additional 15 minutes. Allow to cool.

Meanwhile, melt the butter in a skillet, add the shallots, garlic, and thyme and cook over a low heat, stirring frequently, for 5 minutes. Increase the heat, add the mushrooms and salt and pepper and cook, stirring, for 4–5 minutes until browned. Allow to cool. Sprinkle over the tart case. Beat the sour cream, eggs, Parmesan, and salt and pepper together and pour over the top. Bake for 20–25 minutes until golden and just set. Serve warm with some arugula leaves.

For spinach & feta tart, replace the mushrooms with 2¼ cups frozen leaf spinach, defrosted and squeezed dry. Add to the cooked shallot mixture and spread over the tart shell. Add the sour cream mixture and sprinkle with 4 oz crumbled feta cheese. Continue as above.

tomato & feta tart

Serves **4**

Preparation time **15 minutes**

Cooking time **20 minutes**

12 oz **puff pastry**, defrosted
   if frozen

all-purpose flour, for dusting

3 tablespoons **Pesto** (see
   page 86)

8 oz **baby plum tomatoes,**
   halved

4 oz **feta cheese**, crumbled

4 tablespoons freshly grated
   Parmesan cheese

handful of **basil leaves**

salt and black pepper

Roll the pastry out on a lightly floured work surface to form a rectangle 10 x 14 inches. Using a sharp knife, score a 1 inch border around the edges. Transfer to a baking sheet and spread the pesto over the pastry.

Arrange the tomatoes and feta over the top and sprinkle with the Parmesan. Season with salt and pepper. Bake in a preheated oven, 425°F, for 20 minutes until the pastry is puffed and golden. Remove from the oven and sprinkle with the basil leaves.

For individual tartlets, roll the pastry out to a rectangle 10 x 15 inches. Cut in half lengthwise and then across into 3, to make 6 x 5 inch squares. Divide the pesto and toppings equally between the squares and bake for 15 minutes or until puffed up and golden.

mixed seed soda bread

Makes **1 small loaf**
Preparation time **10 minutes**
Cooking time **40–45 minutes**

spray oil, for greasing
2 cups **whole-wheat**
   all-purpose flour, plus extra
   for dusting and sprinkling
½ cup **sunflower seeds**
2 tablespoons **poppy seeds**
1 teaspoon **baking soda**
1 teaspoon **salt**
1 teaspoon **superfine sugar**
1¼ cups **buttermilk**

Lightly grease a baking sheet with spray oil. Mix the flour, sunflower seeds, poppy seeds, baking soda, salt, and sugar together in a bowl. Make a well in the center, add the buttermilk and gradually work into the flour mixture to form a soft dough.

Turn the dough out on a lightly floured work surface and knead for 5 minutes. Shape into a flattish round. Transfer to the prepared baking sheet. Using a sharp knife, cut a cross in the top of the bread. Sprinkle a little extra flour over the surface.

Bake in a preheated oven, 450°F, for 15 minutes, then reduce the temperature to 400°F, and bake for an additional 25–30 minutes until risen and the loaf sounds hollow when tapped underneath. Allow to cool completely on a cooling rack.

For steel-cut oatmeal soda bread, follow the above recipe, replacing the sunflower seeds with ⅓ cup steel-cut oatmeal. Omit the poppy seeds and continue as above.

chili & corn cornbread

Serves **8–12**
Preparation time **10 minutes**
Cooking time **30–40 minutes**

spray oil, for greasing
¾ cup **all-purpose flour**
1 tablespoon **baking powder**
1¼ cups **medium cornmeal**
1 teaspoon **salt**
3 **eggs**, beaten
1¼ cups **plain yogurt**
4 tablespoons **sunflower oil**
7 oz can **corn kernels**,
   drained
1 large **red chili**, seeded and
   chopped

Lightly grease a 2 lb loaf pan with spray oil and line the base with nonstick parchment paper.

Sift the flour and baking powder into a bowl and stir in the cornmeal and salt. Make a well in the center. Mix the eggs, yogurt, and oil together in a separate bowl. Add to the well and gradually beat into the flour mixture to make a smooth batter. Stir in the corn and chili.

Pour the mixture into the prepared pan. Bake in a preheated oven, 400°F, for 30–40 minutes. Allow to cool in the pan for 5 minutes, then turn out and allow to cool completely on a cooling rack.

For chili & corn muffins, line a 12-hole muffin pan with paper bake cases. Divide the mixture among the paper cases. Bake at 400°F, for 20–25 minutes until risen and golden. Transfer to a cooling rack and allow to cool.

herb & cheese damper

Serves **8**
Preparation time **10 minutes**
Cooking time **30 minutes**

spray oil, for greasing
4 cups **self-rising flour**, plus
   extra for dusting
½ teaspoon **salt**
1 tablespoon chilled **butter**,
   diced
½ cup grated **cheddar cheese**
2 teaspoons chopped
   rosemary
⅔ cup **milk**
⅔ cup **water**

Lightly grease a baking sheet with spray oil. Sift the flour and salt into a bowl. Add the butter and blend with the fingertips until the mixture resembles fine bread crumbs. Stir in the cheddar and rosemary. Make a well in the center, add the milk and measurement water and gradually work into the flour mixture to form a soft dough.

Turn the dough out on a lightly floured work surface and knead gently into a smooth ball. Transfer the dough to the prepared baking sheet and flatten slightly to form a 7 inch round. Using a sharp knife, score the surface into 8 wedges. Bake in a preheated oven, 400°F, for about 30 minutes until risen and the loaf sounds hollow when tapped underneath. Transfer to a cooling rack and allow to cool completely.

For individual rolls, divide the dough into 8 pieces. Shape each piece into a ball and flatten slightly into a round. Brush each one with a little milk and sprinkle with a little extra grated cheddar. Bake at 400°F, for 18–20 minutes until cooked.

eggplant & goat cheese gratin

Serves **6**

Preparation time **10 minutes**

Cooking time **1 hour 10 minutes**

spray oil, for greasing

2 x 13 oz cans **chopped tomatoes**

2 large **garlic cloves**, crushed

4 tablespoons **extra virgin olive oil**

1 teaspoon **superfine sugar**

2 tablespoon chopped **basil**

2 **eggplants**

8 oz **soft goat cheese**, sliced or crumbled

½ cup freshly grated **Parmesan cheese**

salt and black pepper

Lightly grease a 6 cup baking dish with spray oil. Put the tomatoes, garlic, half the oil, sugar, basil, and salt and pepper in a saucepan and bring to a boil. Reduce the heat and simmer for 30 minutes until reduced and thickened.

Cut each eggplant lengthwise into 6 thin slices. Season the remaining oil with salt and pepper, then brush the eggplant slices with the seasoned oil. Cook under a preheated hot broiler for 3–4 minutes on each side until charred and tender.

Arrange one-third of the eggplant slices, overlapping them slightly, in the base of the prepared dish. Add one-third of the tomato sauce and one-third of the goat cheese and Parmesan. Repeat these layers, finishing with the 2 cheeses. Bake in a preheated oven, 400°F, for 30 minutes until bubbling and golden.

For eggplant lasagna, follow the above recipe to the end of the second stage, then set the eggplants and tomato sauce aside. Make 1 quantity Cheese Sauce (see page 90). Layer the eggplants, tomato sauce, and cheese sauce in an 8 cup baking dish, sprinkle 4 tablespoons grated Parmesan over the top and bake as above for 35–40 minutes until bubbling and golden.

potato gratin with pine nut crust

Serves **6**
Preparation time **15 minutes**
Cooking time **1½ hours**

spray oil, for greasing
2 lb small waxy **potatoes**
freshly grated **nutmeg**, to
 taste
2 tablespoons **butter**, diced
¾ cup **milk**
¾ cup **heavy cream**
salt and black pepper

For the pine nut crust
1 cup fresh **whole-wheat
 bread crumbs**
⅛ cup **pine nuts**
¼ cup freshly grated
 Parmesan cheese
1 tablespoon chopped
 parsley

Lightly grease a 4 cup baking dish with spray oil. Peel the potatoes, then cut into wafer-thin slices. Arrange the slices, in overlapping layers, in the prepared dish, seasoning each layer with nutmeg, salt, and pepper and adding small knobs of butter.

Mix the milk and cream together, pour over the potatoes and cover the dish with foil. Bake in a preheated oven, 375°F, for 1 hour until the potatoes are almost tender.

Meanwhile, combine the bread crumbs, pine nuts, Parmesan, and parsley in a bowl.

Remove the foil from the gratin and sprinkle the bread crumb mixture over to form a crust. Bake for an additional 25–30 minutes until the topping is crisp and golden.

For potato & parsnip gratin, thinly slice 1 lb small waxy potatoes and 1 lb parsnips and arrange in alternate layers in a 4 cup baking dish lightly greased with spray oil. Continue as in the recipe above.

four cheese pizza

Makes **2**

Preparation time **20 minutes**, plus rising

Cooking time **20–30 minutes**

4 oz **mozzarella cheese**, sliced

2 oz **taleggio or fontina cheese**, diced

2 oz **Gorgonzola cheese**, crumbled

4 tablespoons freshly grated **Parmesan cheese**

arugula leaves, to serve

For the pizza dough

2 cups **white bread flour**, plus extra for dusting

1 teaspoon **active dry yeast**

1 teaspoon **sea salt**

pinch of **superfine sugar**

⅔ cup **warm water**

1 tablespoon **extra virgin olive oil**

spray oil, for greasing

First make the pizza dough. Sift the flour into a bowl and stir in the yeast, salt, and sugar. Make a well in the center, add the measurement water and oil and gradually work into the flour mixture to form a soft dough.

Lightly grease a bowl with spray oil. Turn the dough out on a lightly floured work surface. Knead for 10 minutes until smooth and elastic. Put in the prepared bowl, cover, and allow to rise in a warm place for 1 hour until doubled in size.

Put a heavy baking sheet on the middle shelf of a preheated oven, 450°F, and heat for 5 minutes. Knock the air out of the dough. Divide in half. Roll one half out to a 10 inch round. Transfer to the heated baking sheet and sprinkle with half the cheeses. Bake for 10–15 minutes until the base is crisp and golden. Serve immediately, topped with arugula leaves. Repeat to make the second pizza.

For cherry tomato & cheese pizza, top each pizza base with 8 halved cherry tomatoes, 4 oz sliced mozzarella, ⅓ cup pitted black olives, and a few basil leaves. Bake as above. Cook the pizzas one at a time for the best results. To serve 4, simply double the quantities.

roasted squash & sage pizza

Makes **2**

Preparation time **20 minutes**, plus rising

Cooking time **45–55 minutes**

spray oil, for greasing

1 quantity **Pizza Dough** (see page 190)

white bread flour, for dusting

1 lb **butternut squash**, peeled

1 **onion**, sliced

2 tablespoons **extra virgin olive oil**

2 **garlic cloves**, finely chopped

pinch of **dried red pepper flakes**

1 tablespoon chopped **sage**

8 oz **mozzarella cheese**, sliced

4 tablespoons freshly grated **Parmesan cheese**

salt and black pepper

Lightly grease a bowl with spray oil. Turn the dough out on a lightly floured work surface. Knead for 10 minutes until smooth and elastic. Put in the prepared bowl, cover, and allow to rise in a warm place for 1 hour until doubled in size.

Meanwhile, cut the squash in half and scoop out and discard the seeds and fibers. Cut into 1 inch dice. Put in a roasting pan, add the onion, half the oil, the garlic, pepper flakes, sage, and salt and pepper and toss well. Roast in a preheated oven, 450°F, for 25 minutes until tender, stirring halfway through.

Put a heavy baking sheet on the middle shelf of the oven and heat for 5 minutes. Knock the air out of the dough. Divide in half. Roll one half out to a 10 inch round. Transfer to the heated baking sheet. Top with half the squash mixture and half the cheeses. Bake for 10–15 minutes until the base is crisp and golden. Serve immediately. Repeat to make the second pizza.

For roasted squash & sage calzone, roll the entire dough out to form a large round 16 inches across. Arrange the squash mixture on one half and top with the cheeses. Dampen the edges with water, fold the remaining dough over the filling, and press the edges together to seal. Bake on a baking sheet at the same temperature as above for 25–30 minutes until puffed and golden.

asparagus & taleggio pizza

Makes **2**
Preparation time **15 minutes**,
  plus rising
Cooking time **20–30 minutes**

spray oil, for greasing
1 quantity **Pizza Dough** (see
  page 190)
white bread flour, for dusting
5 tablespoons **passata**
  (sieved tomatoes)
1 tablespoon ready-made **red
  pesto**
pinch of **salt**
8 oz **taleggio cheese**, sliced
6 oz **slim asparagus**, trimmed
2 tablespoons **olive oil**
black pepper

Lightly grease a bowl with spray oil. Turn the dough out on a lightly floured work surface. Knead for 10 minutes until smooth and elastic. Put in the prepared bowl, cover, and allow to rise in a warm place for 1 hour until doubled in size.

Put a heavy baking sheet on the middle shelf of a preheated oven, 450°F, and heat for 5 minutes. Meanwhile, mix the passata, pesto, and salt together in a bowl.

Knock the air out of the dough. Divide in half. Roll one half out to a 10 inch round. Transfer to the heated baking sheet. Spread half the passata mixture over the pizza base. Top with half the taleggio slices and asparagus and drizzle with half the oil. Bake for 10–15 minutes until the base is crisp and golden. Season with pepper and serve immediately. Repeat to make the second pizza.

For artichoke & buffalo mozzarella pizza, use the same quantity of ready-made green pesto instead of red pesto. Slice 8 oz buffalo mozzarella and use in place of the taleggio and replace the asparagus with the same quantity of drained bottled or canned artichoke hearts in oil. Finish the recipe as above.

goat cheese flatbread pizza

Makes **4**
Preparation time **10 minutes**
Cooking time **7–8 minutes**

4 x 8 inch **Mediterranean flatbreads**
2 tablespoons **sun-dried tomato paste**
10 oz **mozzarella cheese**, sliced
6 **plum tomatoes**, roughly chopped
4 tablespoons **olive oil**
1 **garlic clove**, crushed
small handful of **basil leaves**, roughly torn
4 oz **soft goat cheese**
salt and black pepper

Lay the flatbreads on 2 baking sheets and spread with the sun-dried tomato paste. Top with the mozzarella slices and bake in a preheated oven, 400°F, for 7–8 minutes, until the bases are crisp and the cheese has melted.

Meanwhile, put the tomatoes in a bowl, add the oil, garlic, and basil and season generously with salt and pepper.

Divide the tomato mixture between the flatbreads and crumble over the goat cheese. Serve immediately.

For easy roasted pepper pizza, replace the plum tomatoes with 4 sun-dried tomatoes in oil, drained and roughly chopped, combined with 1 cup drained bottled roasted sweet peppers, and use chopped oregano instead of the basil. After adding the goat cheese, sprinkle the flatbreads with a few pitted black olives and serve.

desserts

rich chocolate mousse

Serves **4**
Preparation time **5 minutes**,
  plus chilling
Cooking time **3–4 minutes**

6 oz **semisweet chocolate**,
  broken into pieces
6 tablespoons **heavy cream**
3 **eggs**, separated
cocoa powder, for dusting

Put the chocolate and cream in a heatproof bowl set over a saucepan of gently simmering water (do not let the bowl touch the water) and stir until the chocolate has melted. Allow to cool for 5 minutes, then beat in the egg yolks one at a time.

Beat the egg whites in a separate clean bowl until stiff, then lightly fold into the chocolate mixture until combined. Spoon the mousse into 4 dessert glasses or cups and chill for 2 hours. Dust with cocoa powder before serving.

For chocolate & orange mousse, follow the recipe above but add the grated zest of 1 large orange and 2 tablespoons Grand Marnier to the melted chocolate and cream. Continue the recipe as above.

poached apricots with pistachios

Serves **4**

Preparation time **10 minutes**,
plus chilling and cooling

Cooking time **8 minutes**

½ cup **superfine sugar**

1¼ cups **water**

2 strips of **lemon peel**

2 **cardamom pods**

1 **vanilla bean**

12 **apricots**, halved and pitted

1 tablespoon **lemon juice**

1 tablespoon **rosewater**

¼ cup **pistachio nuts**, finely
chopped

**vanilla ice cream or Greek-
style yogurt**, to serve
(optional)

Put a large bowl in the freezer to chill. Put the sugar and measurement water in a wide saucepan and heat over a low heat until the sugar has dissolved. Meanwhile, cut the lemon peel into fine strips, crush the cardamom pods, and split the vanilla bean in half. Add the lemon strips, cardamom, and vanilla bean to the pan.

Add the apricots and simmer gently for 5 minutes, or until softened. Remove from the heat, add the lemon juice and rosewater and transfer to the chilled bowl. Allow to cool until required.

Spoon the apricots and a little of the syrup into serving bowls, sprinkle with the pistachio nuts, and serve with ice cream or Greek-style yogurt, if you desire.

For poached peaches with almonds, follow the first stage of the recipe above, but replace the lemon peel with orange peel and the cardamom pods with ½ cinnamon stick. Peel, halve, and pit 4 large peaches, then poach until softened and add orange juice and orange flower water in place of the lemon juice and rosewater. After cooling, serve sprinkled with slivered flaked almonds instead of the pistachio nuts.

apple fritters with blackberry sauce

Serves **4**
Preparation time **15 minutes**
Cooking time **about 10
  minutes**

2 **eggs**
1 cup **all-purpose flour**
4 tablespoons **superfine
  sugar**
⅔ cup **milk**
sunflower oil, for deep-frying
4 **dessert apples**, cored and
  thickly sliced
1 cup **frozen blackberries**
2 tablespoons **water**
confectioners' sugar, for
  dusting

Separate one egg and put the white into one bowl and the yolk and the whole egg into a second bowl. Add the flour and half the superfine sugar to the second bowl. Beat the egg white until if forms soft peaks, then use the same whisk to beat the flour mixture until smooth, gradually beating in the milk. Fold in the egg white.

Pour the oil into a deep, heavy saucepan until it comes one-third of the way up the side, then heat until it reaches 350–375°F, or until a cube of bread browns in 30 seconds. Dip a few apple slices in the batter and turn gently to coat. Lift out one slice at a time and lower carefully into the oil. Deep-fry, in batches, for 2–3 minutes, turning until evenly golden. Remove with a slotted spoon and drain on paper towels.

Meanwhile, put the blackberries, remaining sugar, and measurement water in a small saucepan and heat for 2–3 minutes until hot. Arrange the fritters on serving plates, spoon the blackberry sauce around and dust with a little confectioners' sugar.

For banana fritters with raspberry sauce, use 4 thickly sliced bananas in place of the apples. Use 1¼ cups raspberries instead of the blackberries. Continue with the recipe as above.

caramel apple crumble

Serves **4**
Preparation time **15 minutes**
Cooking time **25 minutes**

spray oil, for greasing
1½ lb **Bramley cooking apples**
⅓ cup **unsalted butter**, diced, plus extra for greasing
3 tablespoons **light brown sugar**
6 whole **cloves**
½ cup **golden raisins**
5 tablespoons **cold water**

For the crumble topping
¾ cup **rolled oats**
¾ cup **all-purpose flour**
½ cup **ground hazelnuts**
¼ cup **light brown sugar**
2 teaspoons **ground cinnamon**
½ cup **unsalted butter**, diced

Lightly grease 4 x 1¼ cup individual baking dishes or cups with spray oil. Peel, core, and thickly slice the apples and put in a saucepan with the butter, sugar, cloves, golden raisins, and measurement water. Cover and cook over a low heat for 5–6 minutes until the apples are just softened. Divide between the prepared dishes or cups.

Put the oats, flour, ground hazelnuts, sugar, and cinnamon in a bowl and stir well until combined. Add the butter and blend with the fingertips until the mixture resembles coarse bread crumbs. Spoon the crumble topping over the apple mixture and bake in a preheated oven, 375°F, for 25 minutes until bubbling and golden.

For peach & blueberry crumble, replace the apples with 1 lb halved, pitted, and sliced peaches and 1¾ cups blueberries, and cook as in the first stage above with 2 tablespoons butter, 2 tablespoons superfine sugar, and 2 tablespoons cold water until just softened. Continue with the recipe as above.

soufflé jelly omelet

Serves **4**
Preparation time **10 minutes**
Cooking time **8–12 minutes**

6 **eggs**, separated
2 teaspoons **vanilla extract**
4 tablespoons **confectioners' sugar**
3 tablespoons **butter**
4 tablespoons **raspberry jelly**
1 cup **raspberries**, defrosted if frozen
1 cup **blueberries**, defrosted if frozen
light cream, to serve

Beat the egg whites in a large bowl until they form soft peaks. Put the yolks, vanilla extract, and 1 tablespoon of the sugar in a separate bowl and use the same whisk to beat them together. Fold a spoonful of the egg whites into the yolks to loosen the mixture, then add the remainder and fold in gently with a large metal spoon.

Melt half the butter in an 8 inch skillet. As soon as it stops foaming, swirl in half the egg mixture and cook over a medium heat for 3–4 minutes until the underside is golden, then transfer to a preheated hot broiler to brown the top lightly. Carefully slide the omelet onto a warmed serving plate and keep warm in a moderate oven. Repeat with the remaining ingredients to make a second omelet.

Dot the omelets with the jelly and berries, then fold in half to enclose the filling. Dust the tops with the remaining sugar, cut in half and serve immediately with cream.

For soufflé marmalade omelet, use the same quantity of orange marmalade instead of the jelly. Peel 4 oranges, cutting off all the pith around the fruit. Remove the segments and discard the membrane and seeds. Arrange the segments, whole or halved on the omelet with the orange marmalade.

broiled fruits with palm sugar

Serves **4**
Preparation time **10 minutes**
Cooking time **6–16 minutes**

2 tablespoons **palm sugar**
grated zest and juice of **1 lime**
2 tablespoons **water**
½ teaspoon cracked **black peppercorns**
1 lb **mixed prepared fruits**, such as pineapple or peach slices or mango wedges

To serve
cinnamon or **vanilla ice cream**
lime slices

Put the sugar, lime zest and juice, measurement water, and peppercorns in a small saucepan and heat over a low heat until the sugar has dissolved. Plunge the base of the pan into ice water to cool.

Brush the cooled syrup over the prepared fruits and cook under a preheated hot broiler for 6–8 minutes on each side, or over a preheated hot gas barbecue or the hot coals of a charcoal barbecue, for 3–4 minutes on each side until charred and tender.

Serve with scoops of cinnamon or vanilla ice cream and lime slices.

For broiled fruit kebabs, cut the prepared fruits into large chunks, thread onto wooden skewers, presoaked in cold water for 30 minutes, and brush with the cooled syrup before cooking as in the recipe above.

tiramisù cheesecake

Serves **8–12**

Preparation time **20 minutes**, plus chilling

Cooking time **50 minutes– 1 hour**

spray oil, for greasing

16 **Savoiardi cookies** (see page 12)

4 tablespoons cold **espresso coffee**

2 cups **cream cheese**

1 cup **mascarpone cheese**

3 **eggs**

½ cup **superfine sugar**

2 tablespoons **Marsala**

1 oz **semisweet chocolate**

Lightly grease a 9 inch square cake pan with spray oil and line with nonstick parchment paper, allowing the paper to overhang the edges. Arrange the Savoiardi cookies, sugar-side up, in the base of the pan, trimming them to fit, if necessary. Brush the cookies with the coffee.

Put the cream cheese, mascarpone, eggs, sugar, and Marsala in a clean bowl. Using an electric beater, beat together until smooth, then pour into the prepared pan and smooth the surface. Grate over the chocolate to cover the surface of the cake.

Bake in a preheated oven, 275°F, for 50 minutes– 1 hour until firm. Allow to cool, then chill for 1 hour. Carefully remove the cheesecake from the pan and cut into slices.

For chocolate cheesecake, melt 4 oz semisweet chocolate, broken into pieces, in a heatproof bowl set over a saucepan of gently simmering water. Follow the recipe above, folding the melted chocolate into the cheese mixture along with 2 tablespoons sifted cocoa powder. Bake as above.

strawberry & lavender crush

Serves **4**
Preparation time **10 minutes**

2¾ cups fresh **strawberries**
2 tablespoons **confectioners'
sugar**, plus extra for dusting
4–5 **lavender flower stems**,
plus extra to decorate
1⅔ cups **Greek-style or
whole milk yogurt**
4 ready-made **meringue
nests**

Reserve 4 small strawberries for decoration. Hull the remainder, put in a bowl with the sugar and mash together with a fork. Alternatively, process the strawberries and sugar in a food processor or blender to a smooth puree. Pull off the lavender flowers from the stems and crumble them into the puree to taste.

Put the yogurt in a bowl, crumble in the meringues, then lightly mix together. Add the strawberry puree and fold together with a spoon until marbled. Spoon into 4 dessert glasses.

Cut the reserved strawberries in half, then use together with the lavender flowers to decorate the desserts. Lightly dust with confectioners' sugar and serve immediately.

For peach & rosewater crush, peel, halve, and pit 3 peaches, then roughly chop and mash or process in a food processor or blender with 2 tablespoons honey and 2 teaspoons rosewater. Continue with the recipe as above, but decorate the desserts with crystallized rose petals.

summer berry sorbet

Serves **2**

Preparation time **5 minutes**, plus freezing

1⅔ cups **frozen mixed summer berries**

5 tablespoons **spiced berry cordial**

2 tablespoons **Kirsch**

1 tablespoon **lime juice**

Put a shallow plastic container in the freezer to chill. Process the frozen berries, cordial, Kirsch, and lime juice in a food processor or blender to a smooth puree. Be careful not to over-process, as this will soften the mixture too much.

Spoon into the chilled container and freeze for at least 25 minutes. Spoon into serving bowls and serve.

For raspberry sorbet, replace the main recipe ingredients with frozen raspberries, elderflower cordial, crème de cassis, and lemon juice. Use the same quantities and method as the summer berry sorbet.

banana & fig phyllo pastry

Serves **4**
Preparation time **15 minutes**
Cooking time **15 minutes**

6 large sheets of **phyllo pastry**
¼ cup **unsalted butter**, melted
4 **bananas**, sliced
6 **dried figs**, sliced
2 tablespoons **superfine sugar**
grated zest of ½ **lemon**
½ teaspoon ground **cinnamon**
thick heavy cream or **Greek-style yogurt**, to serve

Cut the pastry sheets in half crosswise. Lay one sheet flat on a baking sheet and brush with melted butter, top with a second sheet and again brush with melted butter. Repeat with the remaining sheets.

Arrange the banana and fig slices over the pastry. Combine the sugar, lemon zest, and cinnamon, then sprinkle over the fruit and drizzle over any remaining melted butter.

Bake in a preheated oven, 400°F, for 15 minutes until the pastry is crisp and the fruit golden. Serve hot with cream or Greek-style yogurt.

For spiced apple phyllo pastry, prepare the phyllo pastry base as in the recipe above. Core and quarter 2 apples and cut into wafer-thin slices. Arrange the slices over the pastry in overlapping rows. Drizzle over 2 tablespoons melted butter and sprinkle with 2 tablespoons superfine sugar mixed with 1 teaspoon ground cinnamon. Bake as above for 20 minutes.

bananas with toffee sauce

Serves **4**
Preparation time **5 minutes**
Cooking time **5 minutes**

4 **bananas**
½ cup **unsalted butter**
**ground cinnamon or freshly
  grated nutmeg,** to
  decorate (optional)
vanilla ice cream, to serve

For the toffee sauce
½ cup **palm sugar**
½ cup **heavy cream**
lime juice, to taste

Peel the bananas and cut into quarters or in half lengthwise. Melt the butter in a skillet, add the bananas and cook over a medium-high heat for about 30 seconds on each side until lightly golden. Remove with a slotted spoon and transfer to a warmed dish.

Stir the sugar and cream into the pan and heat over a low heat until the sugar has dissolved. Simmer gently for 2–3 minutes until thickened. Add lime juice to taste.

Serve the bananas drizzled with the toffee sauce and with a scoop of vanilla ice cream. Sprinkle with cinnamon or nutmeg to decorate, if you desire.

For pineapple with toffee sauce, peel a ripe fresh pineapple, removing the "eyes," then slice into rings. Lay the rings on a cutting board and remove the central cores with an apple corer. Cook the pineapple rings in the same way as the bananas and continue with the recipe as above.

caramelized clementines

Serves **4**
Preparation time **10 minutes**,
  plus cooling
Cooking time **15 minutes**

1 cup **granulated sugar**
1 cup **cold water**
6 tablespoons **boiling water**
8 **clementines**, peeled
3 whole **star anise**
cream or crème fraîche,
  to serve

Put the sugar and cold measurement water in a small saucepan and heat over a low heat, without stirring, until the sugar has completely dissolved. Don't be tempted to stir the mixture or the sugar will harden—tilt the pan to mix the sugar, if needed. Increase the heat and boil for 10 minutes, or until just turning pale golden.

Remove the pan from the heat and add the boiling measurement water, a tablespoon at a time, standing well back after each addition as it will spit. Tilt the pan to mix, heating gently if needed.

Put the clementines in a heatproof bowl with the star anise, then pour over the hot syrup and allow to cool for 3–4 hours. Stir the clementines and transfer to a serving dish. Serve with cream or crème fraîche.

For herb-scented caramelized clementines, use 3 fresh rosemary sprigs or 2 bay leaves instead of the star anise. Tuck the herbs under the clementines in the dish before adding the syrup.

brioche pudding with ice cream

Serves **4**
Preparation time **45 minutes**,
   plus infusing, cooling,
   freezing, and soaking
Cooking time **40 minutes**

8 slices of **brioche**
3 **eggs**, lightly beaten
¼ cup **superfine sugar**
1 cup **milk**
1 cup **heavy cream**
½ teaspoon ground **mixed spice**
2 tablespoons **butter**, melted
1 tablespoon **demerara sugar**

For the ice cream
3 cups **heavy cream**
1 **vanilla bean**, split
5 **egg yolks**
½ cup **maple syrup**

First make the ice cream. Put the cream and vanilla bean in a saucepan and heat to boiling point. Remove from the heat and allow to infuse for 20 minutes. Scrape the seeds from the bean into the cream.

Beat the egg yolks and maple syrup together in a bowl, stir in the cream, and return to the pan. Heat gently, stirring, until the custard thickens to coat the back of a wooden spoon. Don't allow to boil. Let cool. Freeze in a plastic container, beating every hour, for 5 hours, or until frozen.

Cut the brioche slices diagonally into quarters to form triangles. Arrange, overlapping, in 4 x 1 cup baking dishes. Beat the eggs, superfine sugar, milk, cream, and spice in a separate bowl. Pour over the brioche slices, pushing them down so that they are almost covered. Drizzle over the butter and sprinkle with the demerara sugar. Allow to soak for 30 minutes.

Set the baking dishes in a large roasting pan. Pour in enough boiling water to come halfway up the sides of the dishes. Bake in a preheated oven, 350°F, for 30 minutes until set and the top is lightly golden. Serve with the ice cream.

For classic bread & butter pudding, replace the brioche slices with white bread. Butter one side, cut diagonally in half and arrange in a 6 cup baking dish. Pour over the custard and bake for 45–50 minutes until set.

orange palmiers with plums

Serves **4**
Preparation time **20 minutes**
Cooking time **10 minutes**

1 sheet of ready-rolled frozen
  puff pastry, about 10 inches
  square, defrosted
1 **egg**, beaten
3 tablespoons **light brown
  sugar**
finely grated zest of ½ **orange**
spray oil, for greasing
6 tablespoons **orange juice**
¼ cup **superfine sugar**
13 oz **plums**, pitted and sliced
confectioners' sugar, for
  dusting
sour cream, to serve

Brush the pastry with some of the beaten egg, then sprinkle with the brown sugar and orange zest. Roll one edge of the pastry until it reaches the center. Do the same from the opposite edge until both rolls meet.

Brush the pastry with more beaten egg, then cut into 8 thick slices. Lightly grease a baking sheet with spray oil. Arrange the pastry slices, cut side-up, on the prepared baking sheet. Bake in a preheated oven, 400°F, for 10 minutes until well risen and golden.

Meanwhile, put the orange juice and superfine sugar in a saucepan. Add the plums and cook, stirring, over a medium heat for 5 minutes.

Sandwich the palmiers together in pairs with the plums, dust with confectioners' sugar and serve with a spoonful of sour cream.

For seasonal fruit palmiers, instead of plums, use the best seasonal ingredients. Chop 1 lb fresh rhubarb, or pit and slice 13 oz greengages. Use 3½ cups raspberries, according to availability. Continue the recipe as above.

very berry fruit salad

Serves **4**
Preparation time **10 minutes**,
  plus cooling
Cooking time **10 minutes**

3 **oranges**
¼ cup **granulated sugar**
1 **vanilla bean**, split
1 **cinnamon stick**, lightly
  bruised
1⅔ cups fresh **strawberries**
1 cup fresh **cherries**
1 cup fresh **raspberries**
1 cup fresh **blueberries**

Squeeze the juice from the oranges into a measuring cup and make up to 1¼ cups with cold water. Put in a saucepan with the sugar, vanilla bean, and cinnamon stick. Heat over a low heat, stirring, until the sugar has dissolved, then simmer gently for 5 minutes until a light syrup is reached.

Remove from the heat and allow to cool completely. Remove the vanilla bean and cinnamon stick.

Hull and halve the strawberries, then put in a large bowl with the remaining berries and pour over the syrup. Stir well and allow to marinate at room temperature for 30 minutes.

For fragrant berry & rosewater salad, put 1¼ cups cold water in a saucepan with ⅓ cup superfine sugar and 1 lightly bruised cinnamon stick. Heat over a low heat, stirring, until the sugar has dissolved, then simmer for 5 minutes. Remove the cinnamon stick, then take the saucepan off the heat and allow to cool. Stir in 1 tablespoon rosewater and the berries.

cherry & cinnamon zabaglione

Serves **4**
Preparation time **10 minutes**
Cooking time **12–15 minutes**

4 **egg yolks**
½ cup **superfine sugar**
⅔ cup **cream sherry**
large pinch of ground
  cinnamon
14 oz can **black cherries**
  in syrup
2 **amaretti cookies**,
  crumbled, to decorate

Pour 2 inches of water into a medium saucepan and bring to a boil. Cover with a large heatproof bowl, making sure that the water does not touch the base of the bowl. Reduce the heat so that the water is simmering, then add the egg yolks, sugar, sherry, and cinnamon to the bowl. Beat for 5–8 minutes until very thick and foamy, and the custard leaves a trail when the beater is lifted above the mixture.

Drain off some of the cherry syrup then tip the cherries and just a little of the syrup into a small saucepan. Warm through, then spoon into 4 dessert glasses.

Pour the warm zabaglione over the top and decorate with the amaretti cookies. Serve immediately.

For apricot & vanilla zabaglione, replace the sherry with Marsala, omit the cinnamon, and add 2 drops vanilla extract and the grated zest of ½ lemon to the egg yolks. Use canned apricots instead of the black cherries. Continue the recipe as above.

rhubarb, pear, & marzipan crumble

Serves **4**
Preparation time **20 minutes**
Cooking time **35–40 minutes**

13 oz **trimmed rhubarb**,
 thinly sliced
1 ripe **pear**, peeled, cored,
 and sliced
½ cup **superfine sugar**
1 cup **all-purpose flour**
¼ cup **butter**, diced
1 cup **marzipan**, coarsely
 grated
slivered almonds, for
 sprinkling
custard, to serve

Put the rhubarb and pear into a 5 cup ovenproof pie dish with half the sugar.

Put the remaining sugar in a food processor, add the flour and butter and process until the mixture resembles fine bread crumbs. Alternatively, put the ingredients into a bowl, add the butter and blend with the fingertips until the mixture resembles fine bread crumbs. Stir in the marzipan.

Spoon over the fruit and sprinkle with a few slivered almonds. Cook in a preheated oven, 350°F, for 35–40 minutes until golden brown, checking after 15–20 minutes and covering with foil to prevent overbrowning if necessary. Serve hot with custard.

For plum, apple, & marzipan crumble, replace the rhubarb with 1 lb halved, pitted ripe plums and the pear with a large peeled, cored, and sliced cooking apple. Continue the recipe as above. The crumble mix can be made in bulk and stored in a plastic bag in the freezer until needed.

sweet wonton millefeuille

Makes **12**

Preparation time **10 minutes**, plus cooling

Cooking time **3 minutes**

2 tablespoons **superfine sugar**

½ teaspoon ground **cinnamon**

9 **wonton skins**

2 tablespoons **unsalted butter**, melted

½ cup **mascarpone cheese**

1–2 tablespoons **confectioners' sugar**, plus extra for dusting

1 teaspoon **lemon juice**

⅔ cup fresh **strawberries**, hulled and sliced

Mix the superfine sugar and cinnamon together. Cut the wonton skins into quarters, brush with the melted butter and coat with a layer of the spiced sugar.

Put on a baking sheet and bake in a preheated oven, 400°F, for 2–3 minutes until crisp and golden. Allow to cool on a cooling rack.

Beat the mascarpone with the confectioners' sugar and lemon juice in a bowl and spread a little over 12 of the crisp wontons. Top with half the strawberry slices. Repeat the process with another 12 wontons and the remaining mascarpone mixture and strawberries to make a second layer. Put the remaining wontons on top and dust with a little extra confectioners' sugar. Serve with glasses of champagne, if you desire.

For sweet berry millefeuille, use raspberries or blackberries instead of the strawberries, and replace the mascarpone with ⅔ cup thick yogurt.

index

acknowledgments

Executive editor: Nicola Hill
Editor: Ruth Wiseall
Deputy creative director: Karen Sawyer
Designer: Janis Utton
Photographer: Ian Wallace
Food and props stylist: Louise Pickford
Production manager: Nigel Reid

Special photography: © Octopus Publishing Group
Limited/Ian Wallace
Other photography: © Octopus Publishing Group
Limited/William Lingwood 55, 65, 79, 93, 147, 153,
195, 197, 205, 209, 215, 223, 227, 231, 233; /Lis
Parsons 37; /William Shaw 43, 175